I is for Impressionism

Nicol Valentin

little piggy press
An Imprint of Primrose Publishers

Copyright © 2021 Nicol Valentin All rights reserved.

No part of this book may be reproduced or transmitted in any form or by any means, including but not limited to information storage and retrieval systems, electronic, mechanical, photocopy, recording, etc. without written permission from the copyright holder.

Published by Primrose Publishing

visit the author at nicolvalentin.com

Dedicated to my crazy, creative, and wonderful children

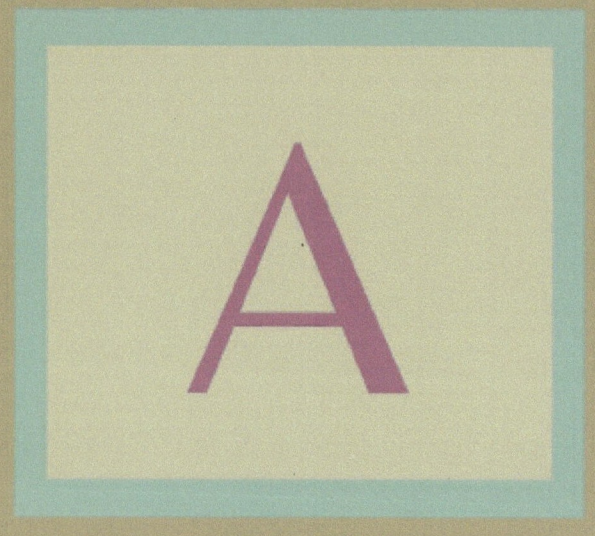

is for apples

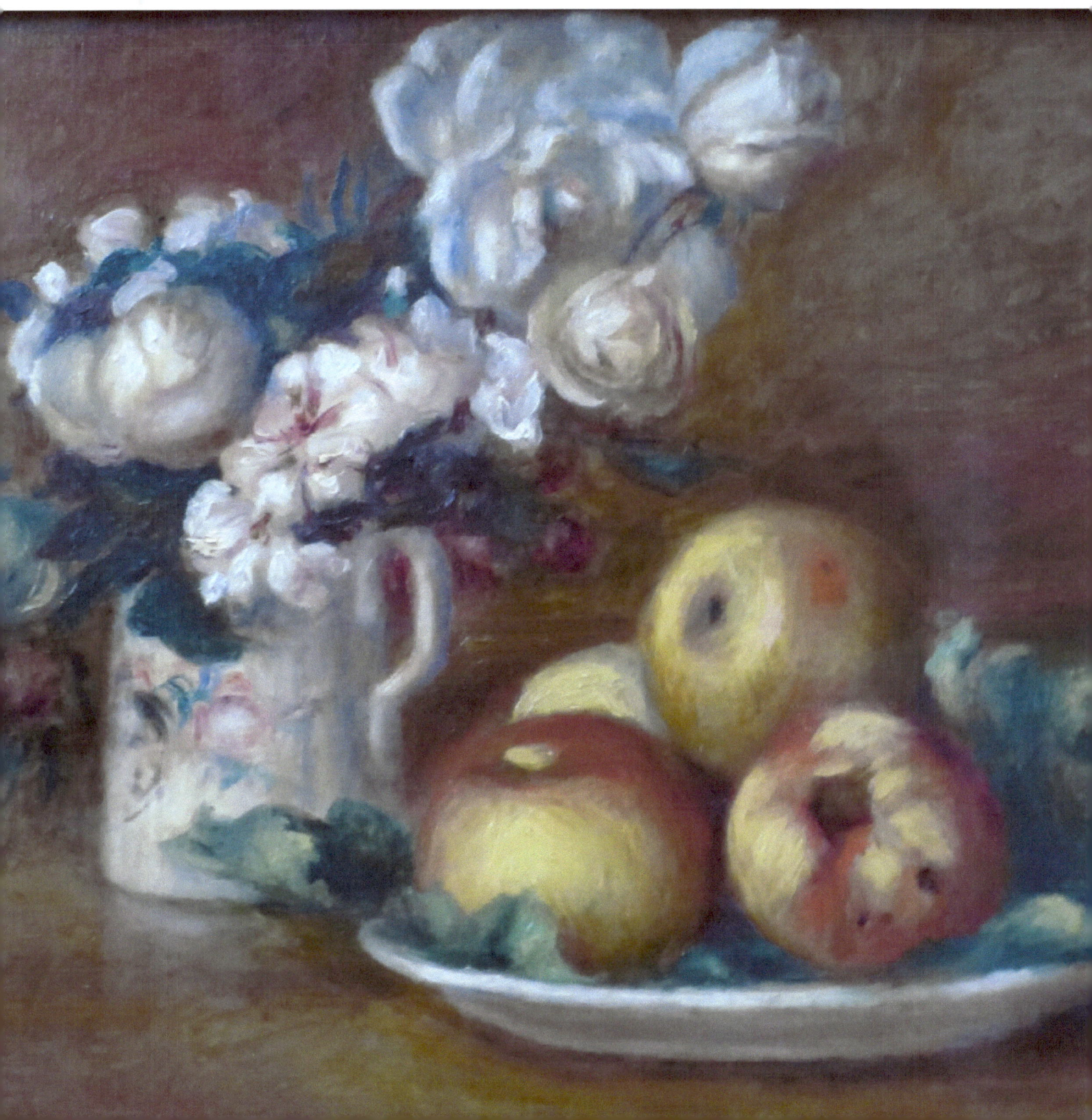

B

is for bath

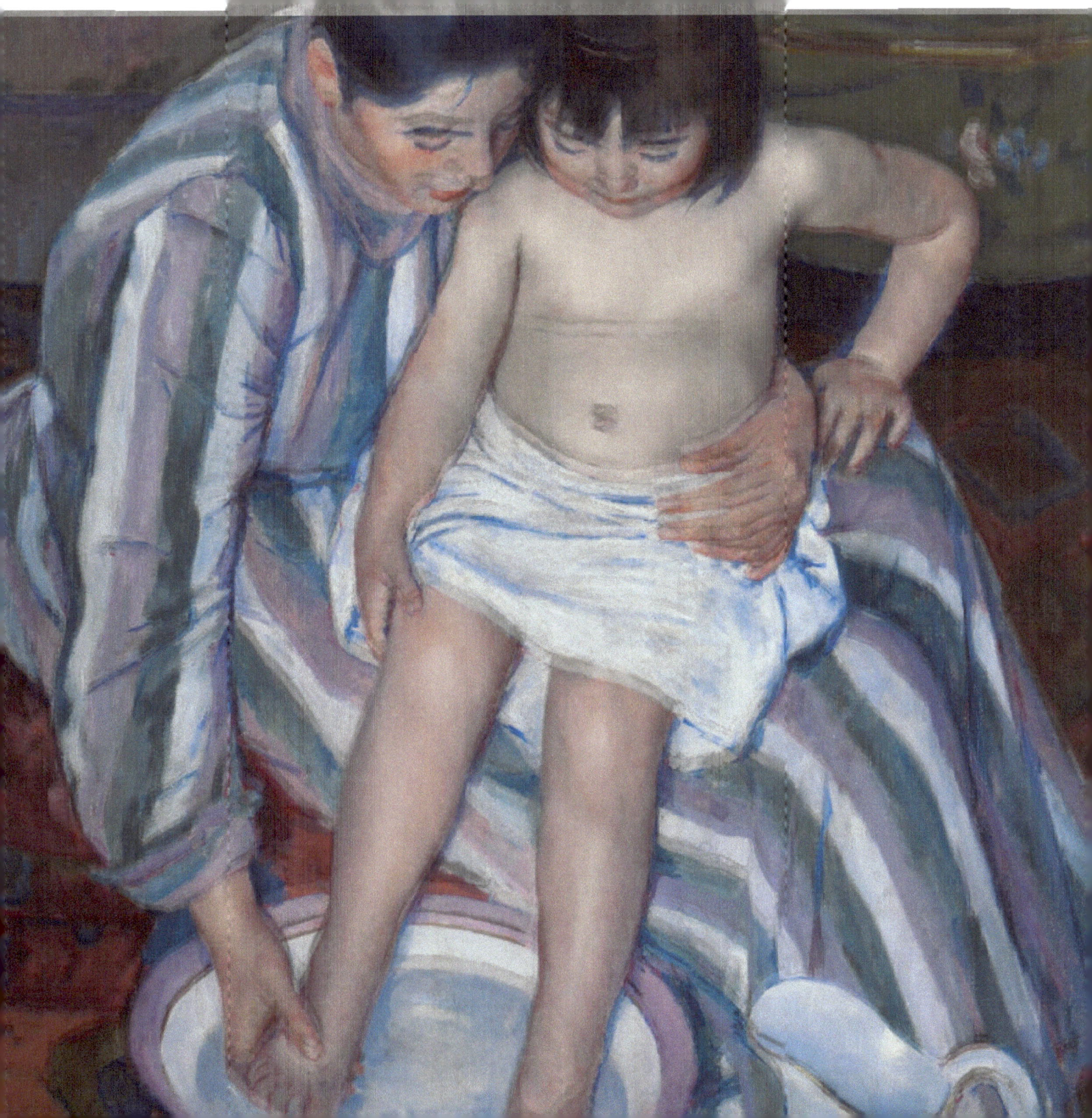

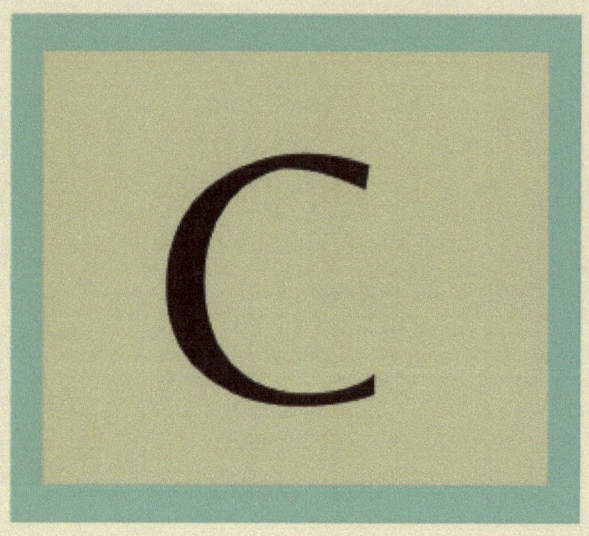

is for cradle

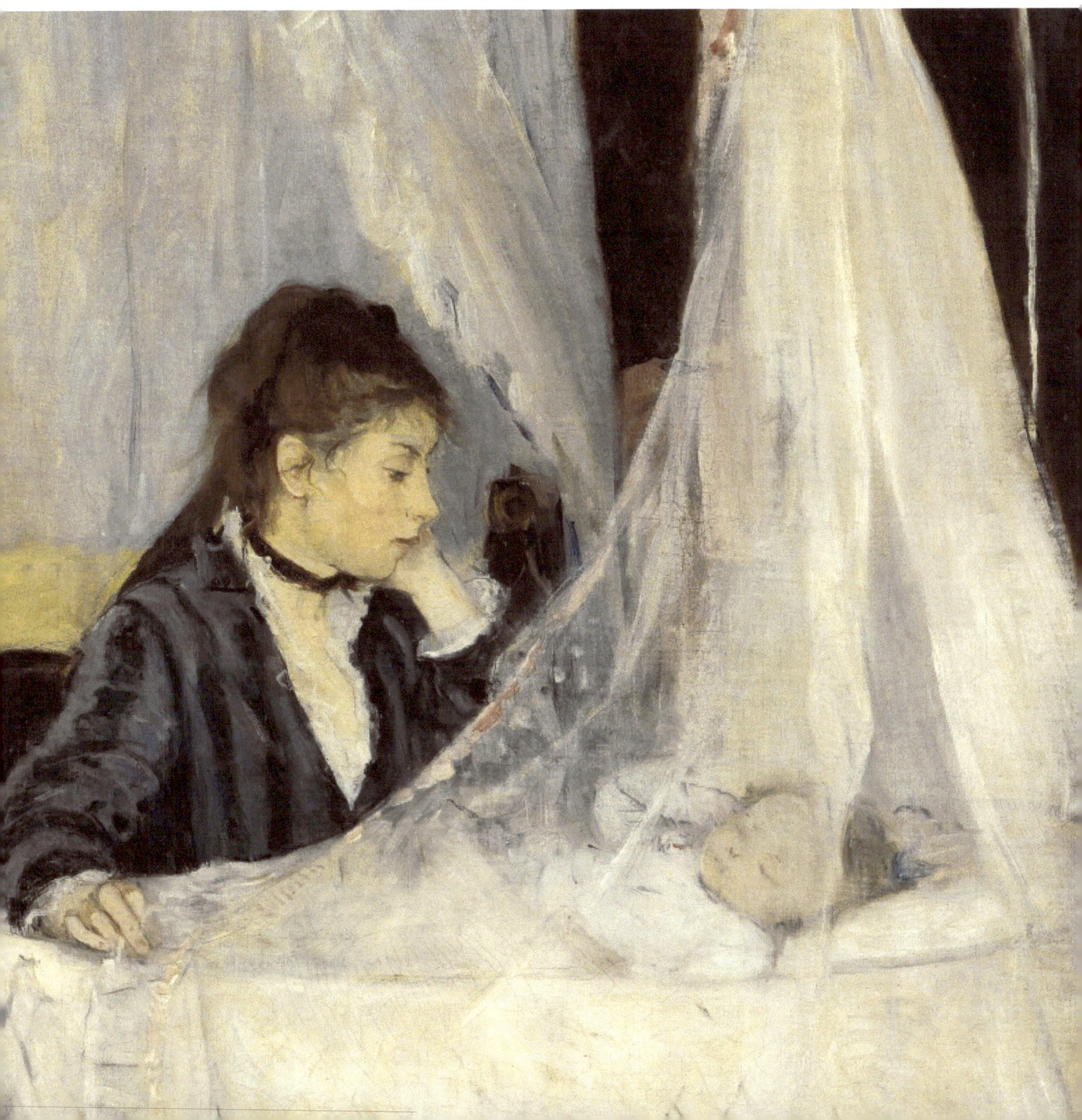

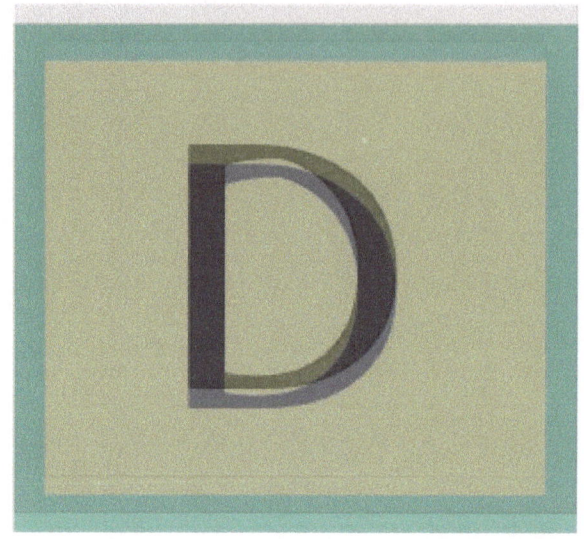

is for dinner

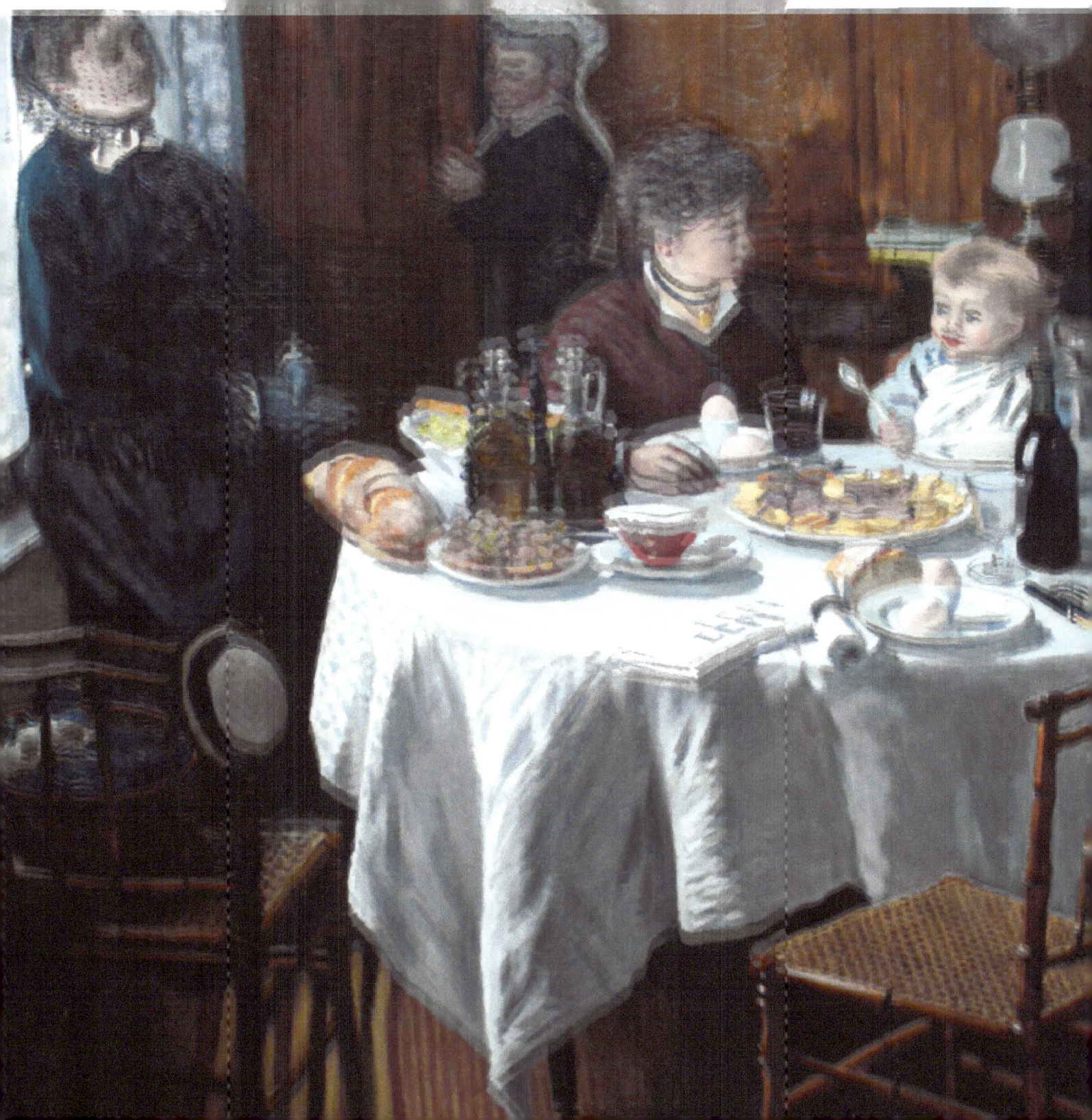

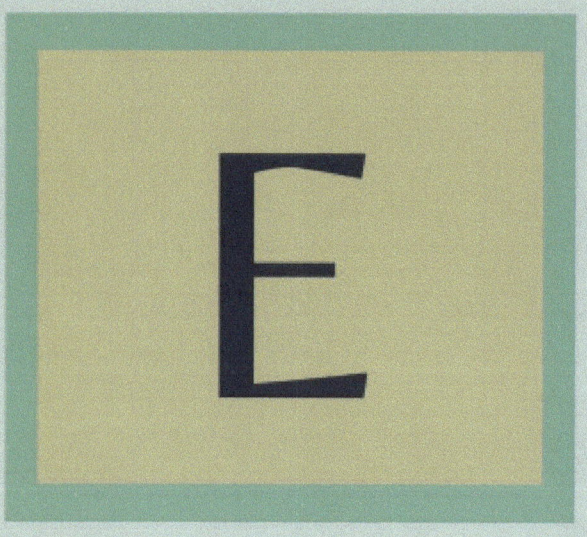

is for engine

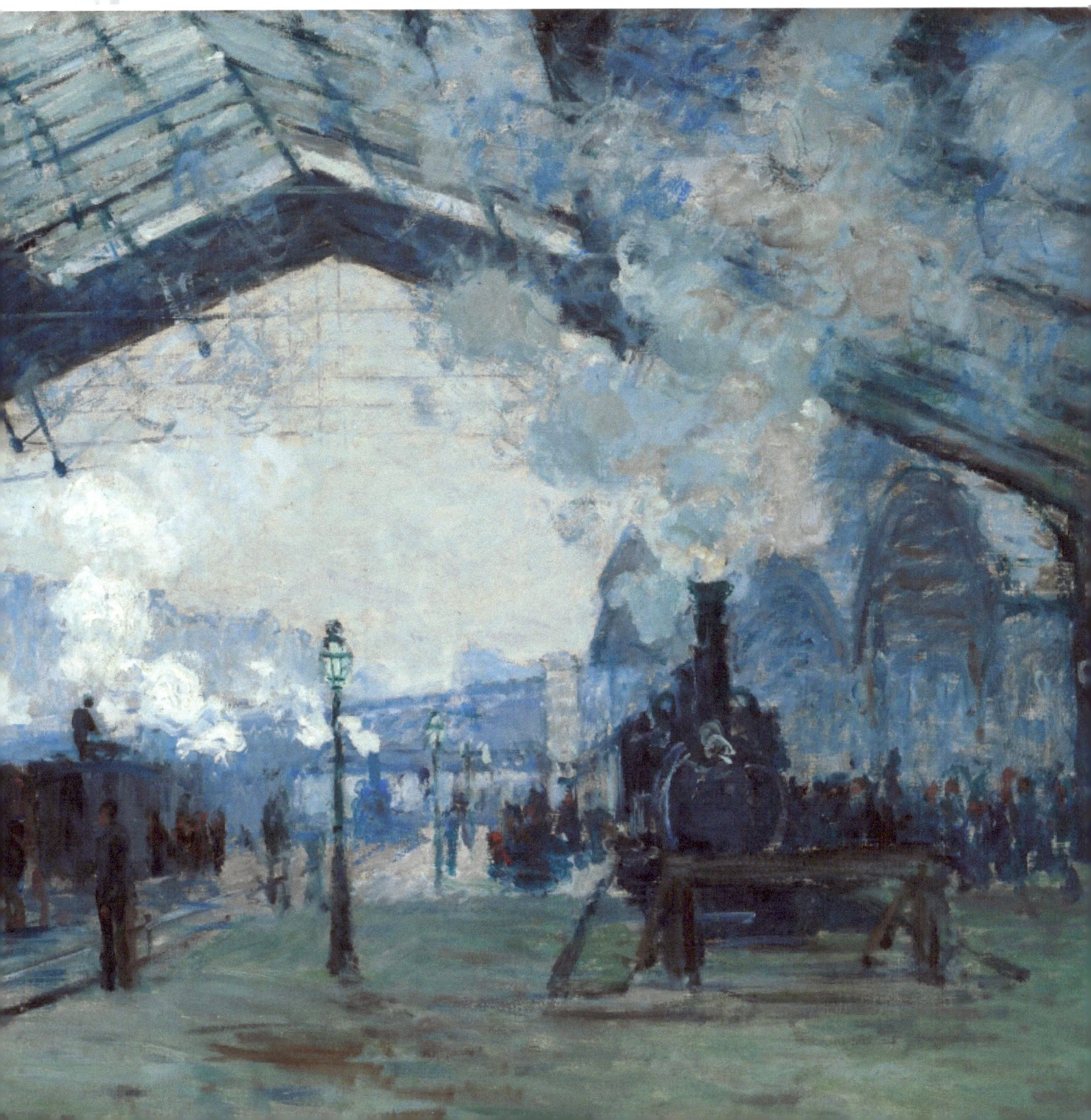

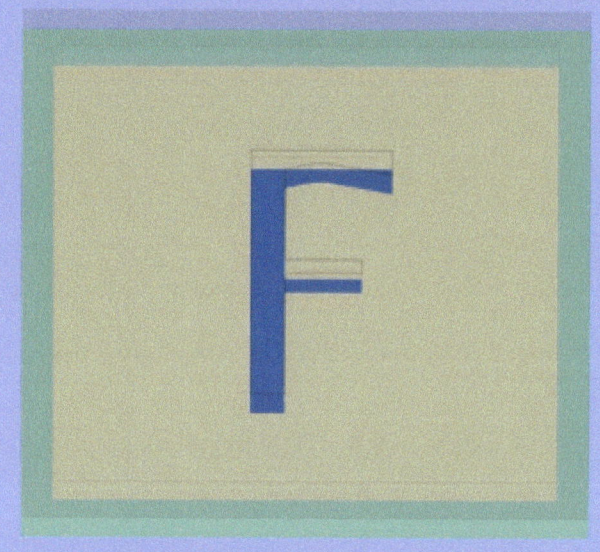

is for flowers

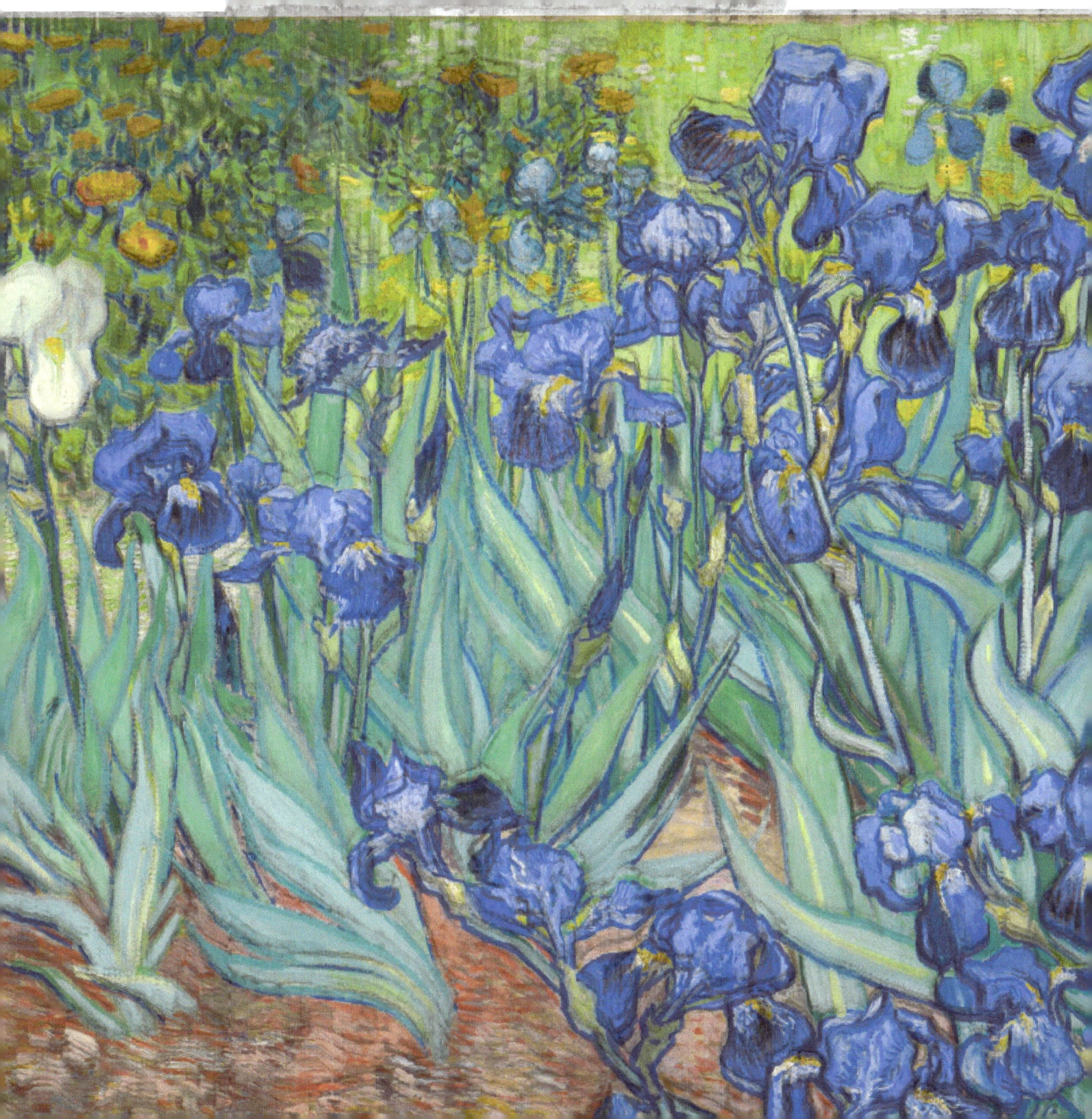

G

is for garden

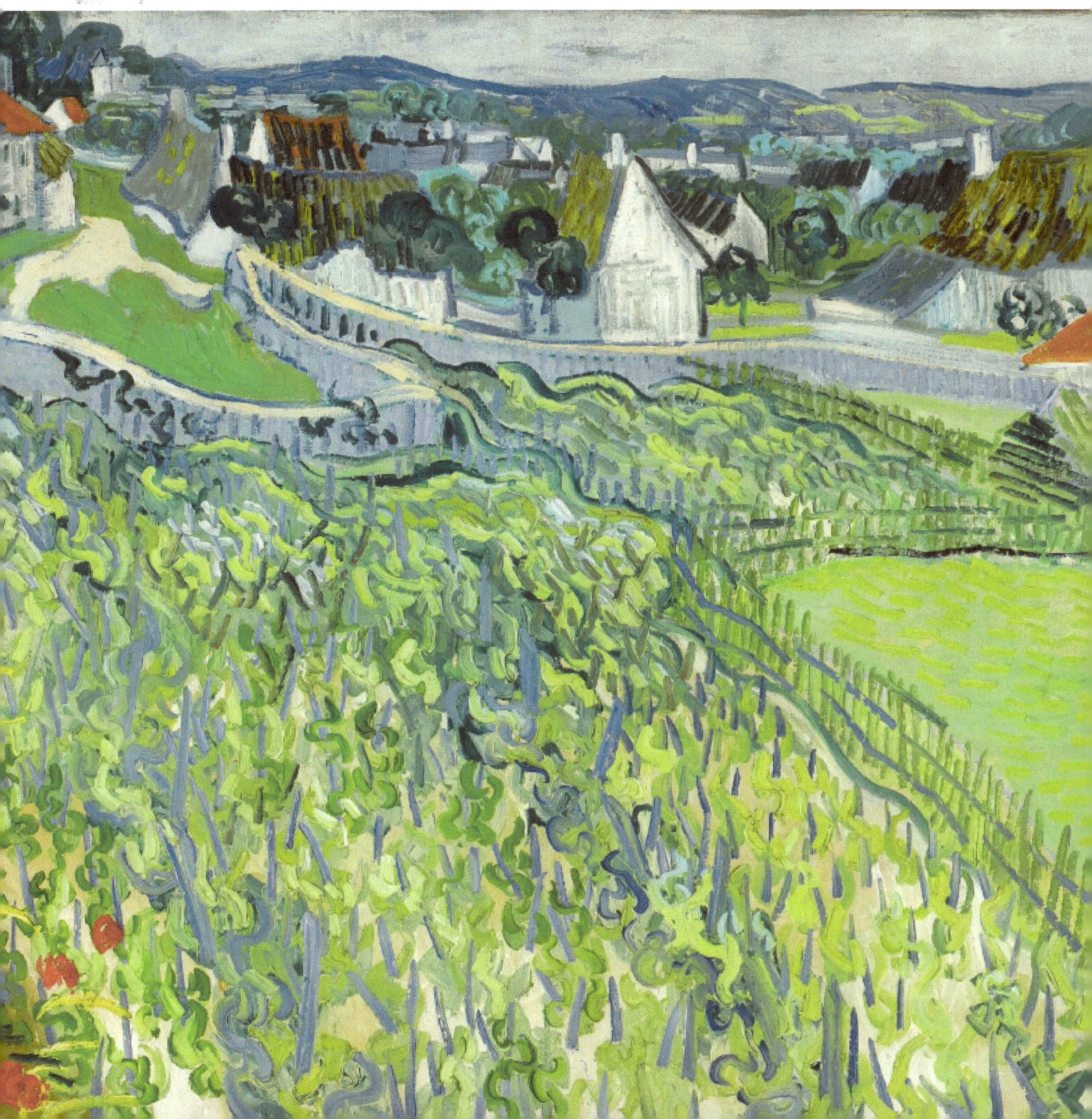

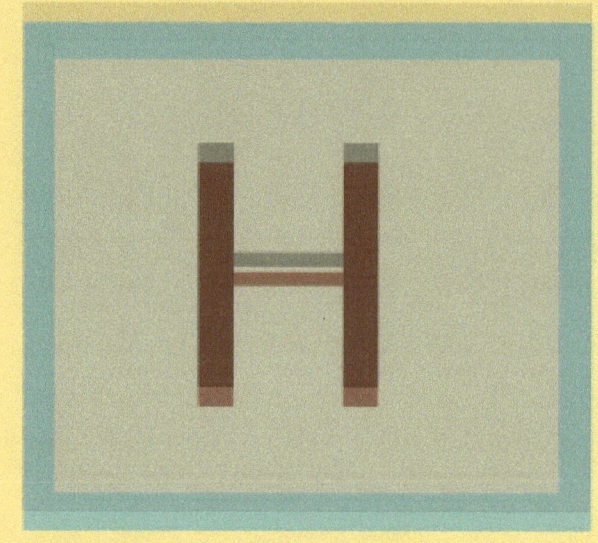

is for haystack

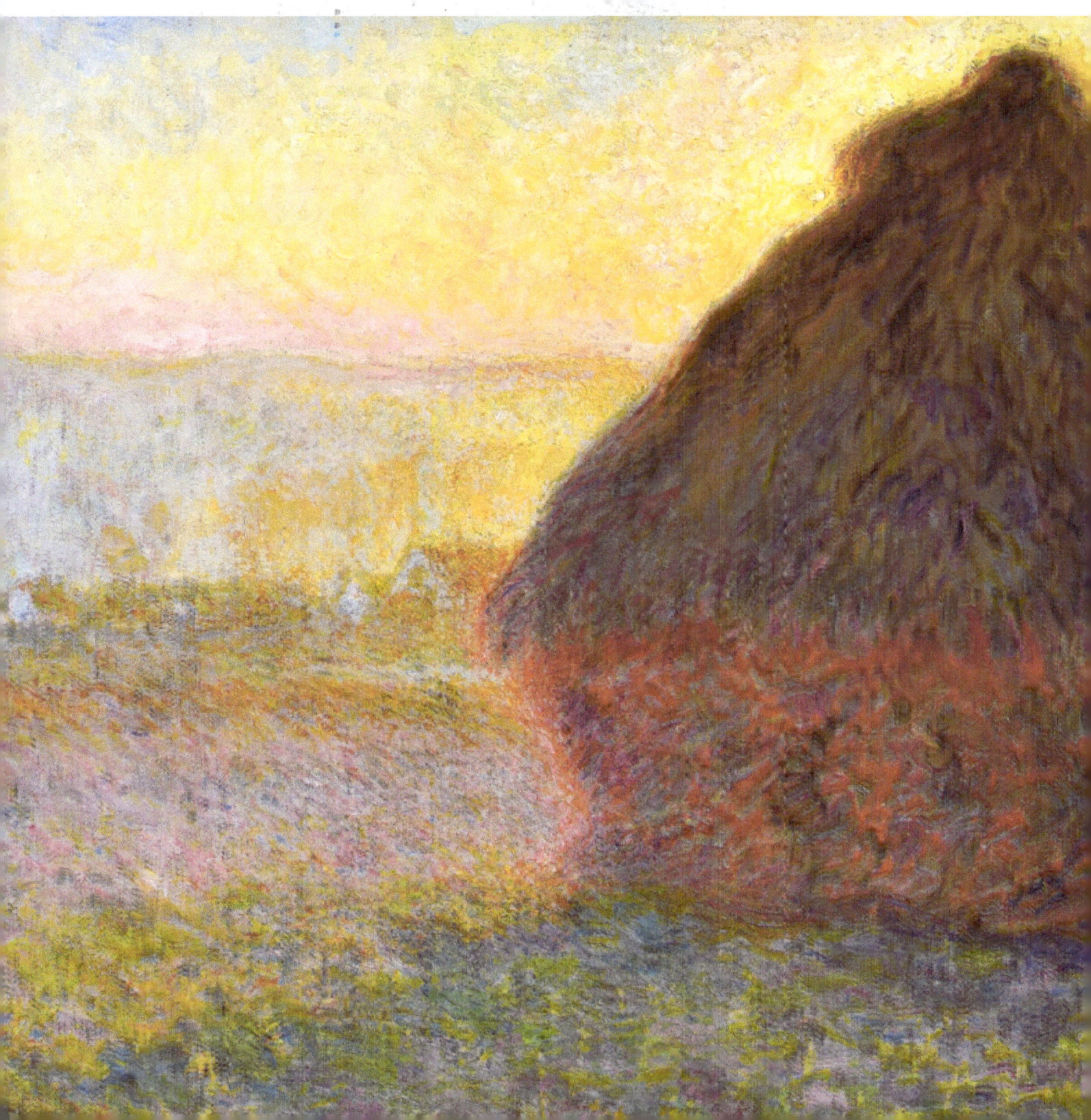

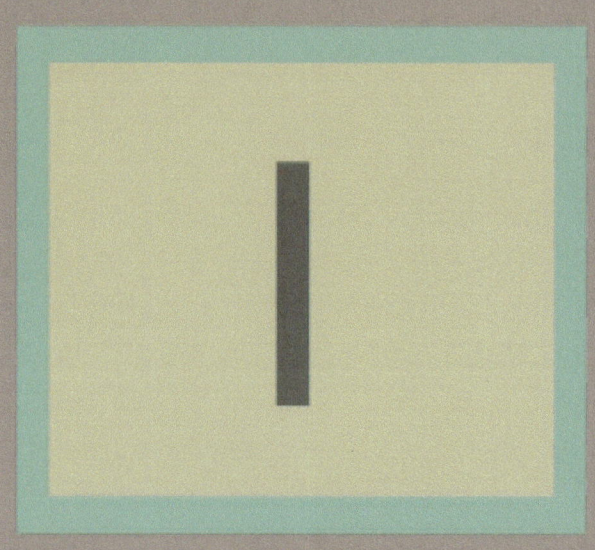

is for impression

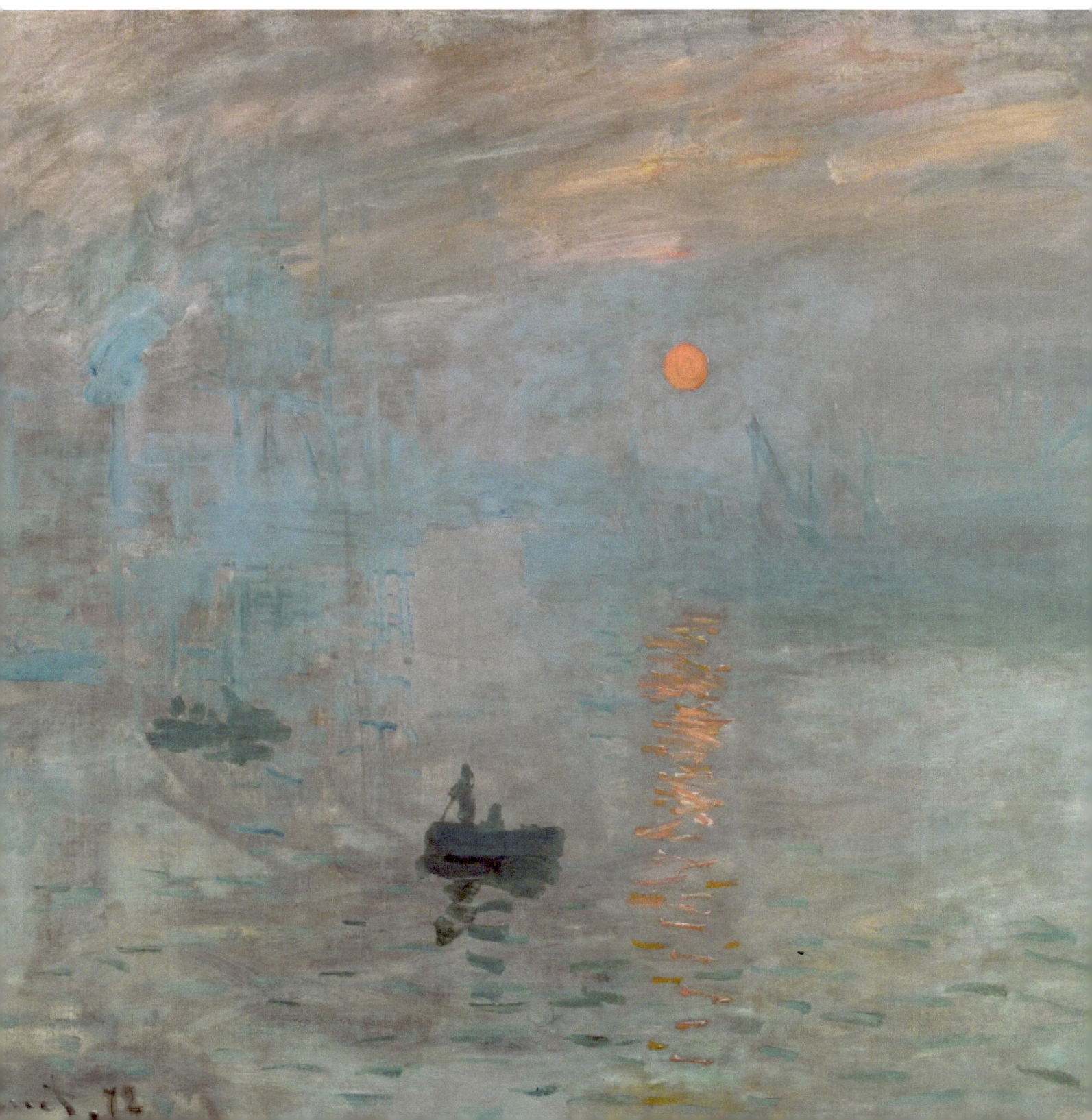

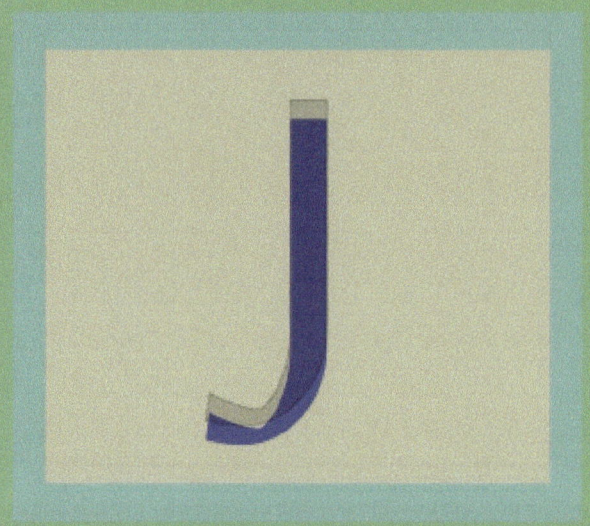

is for jacket

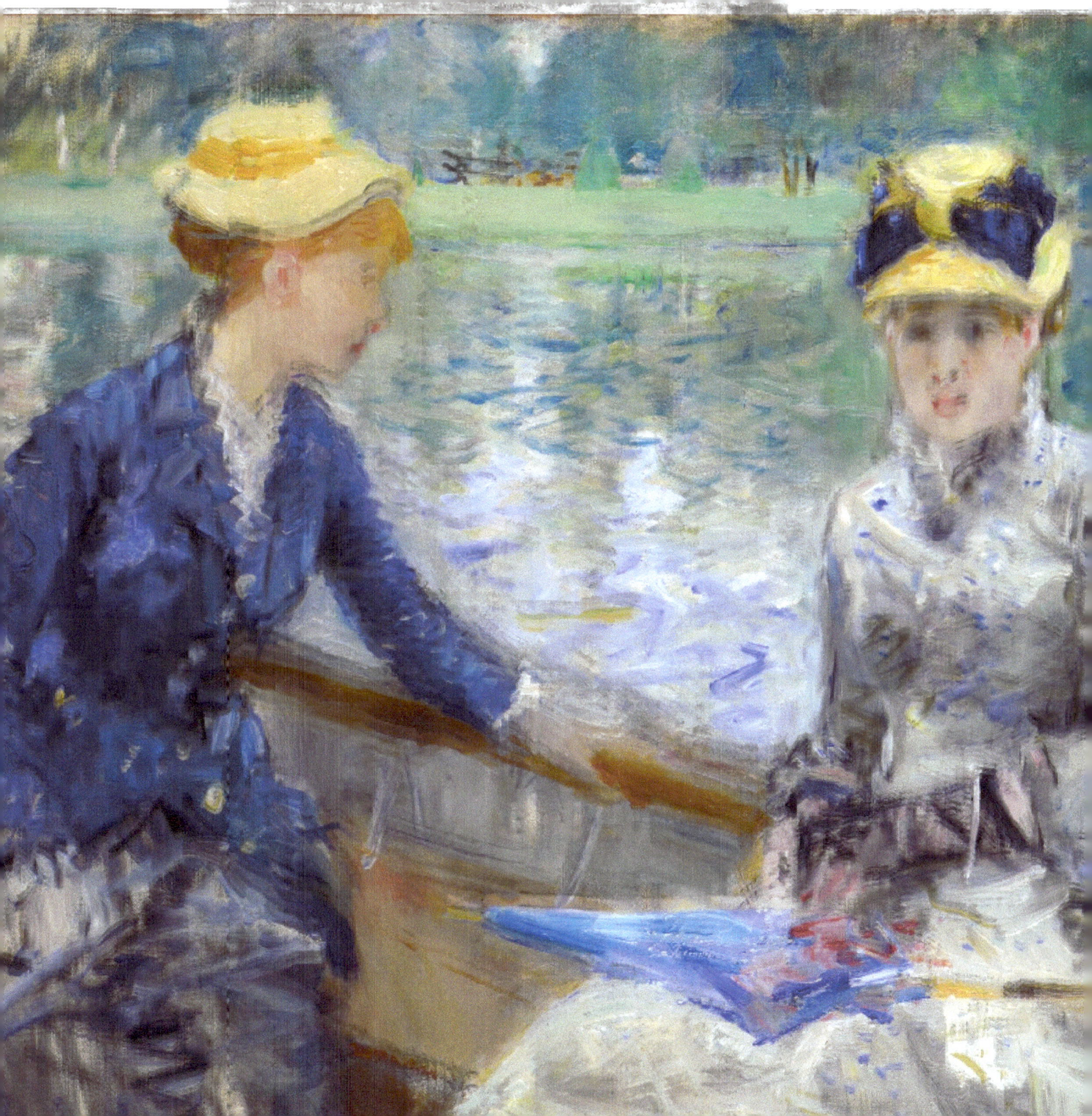

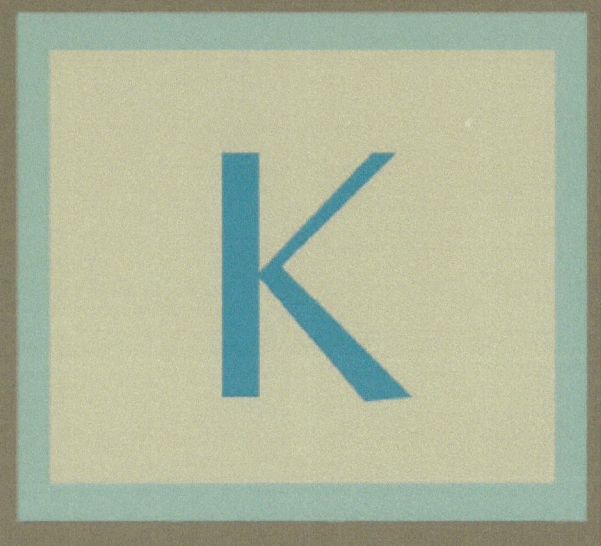

is for kitchen

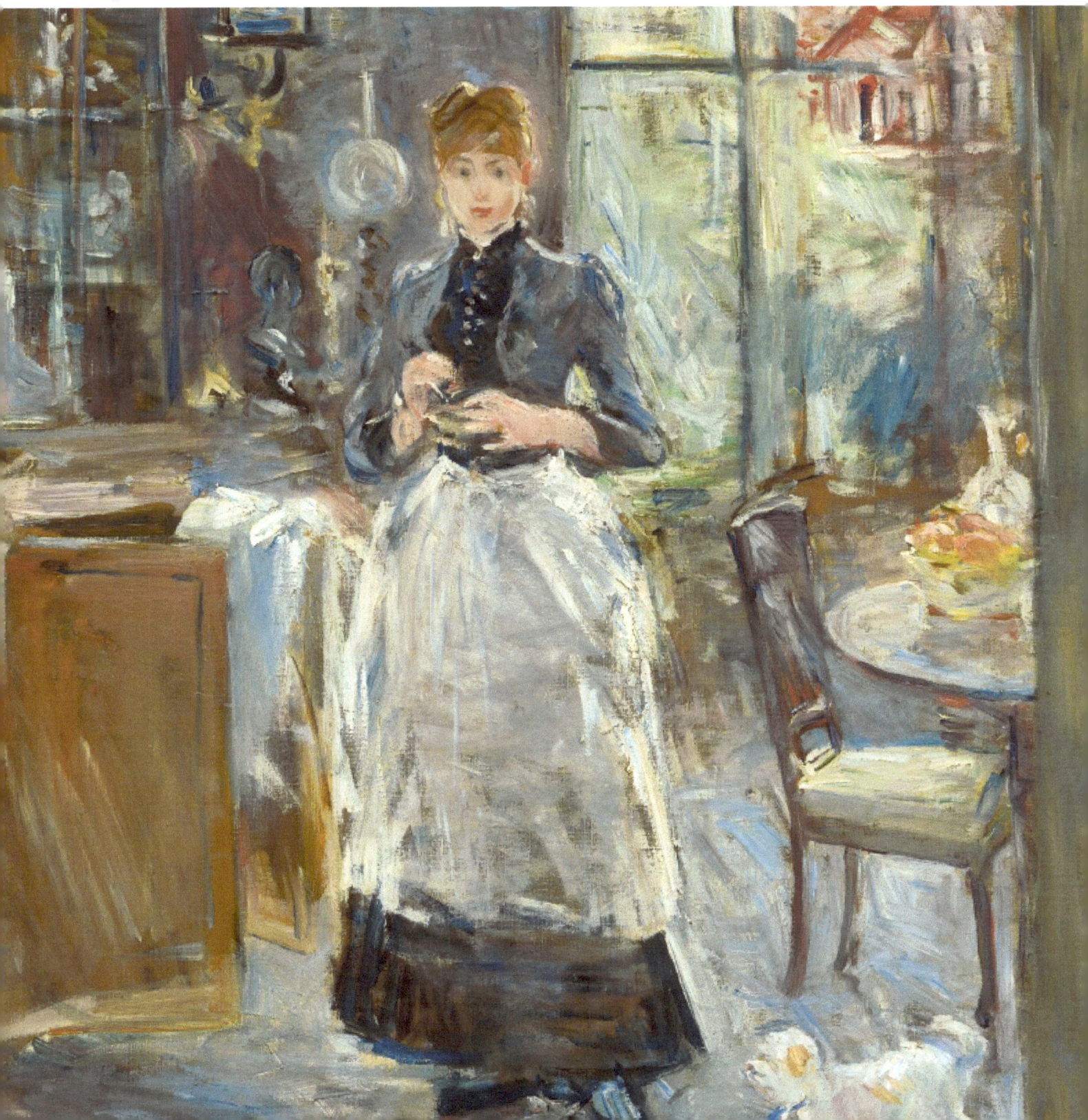

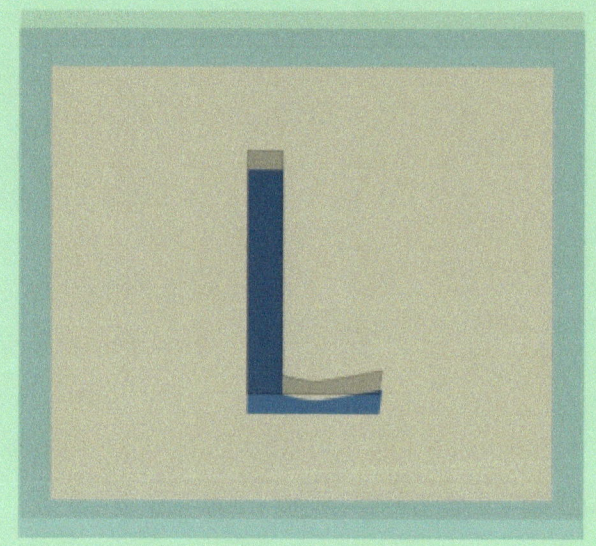

is for lemon

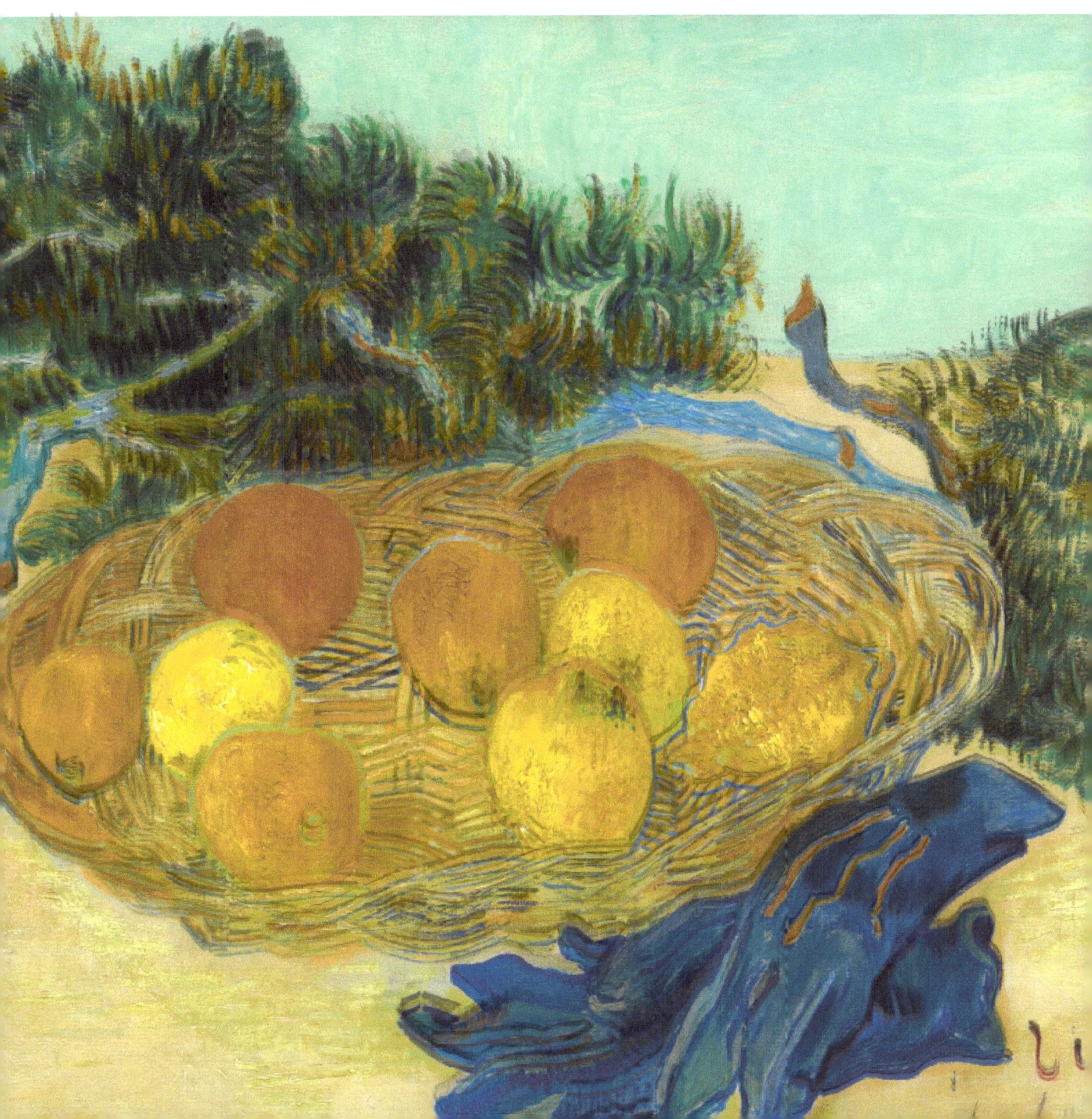

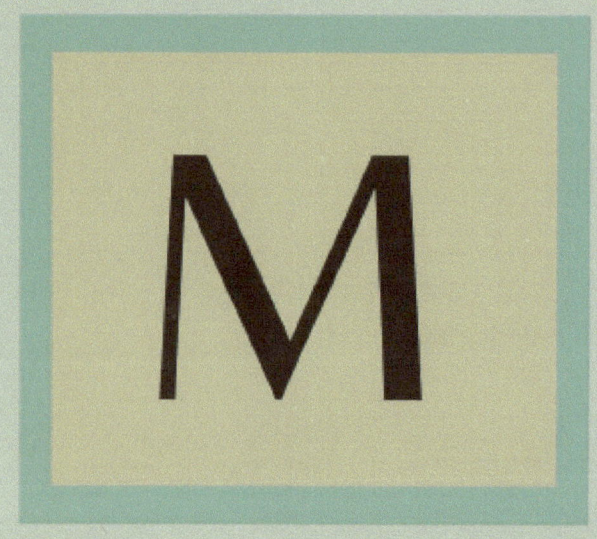

is for meadow

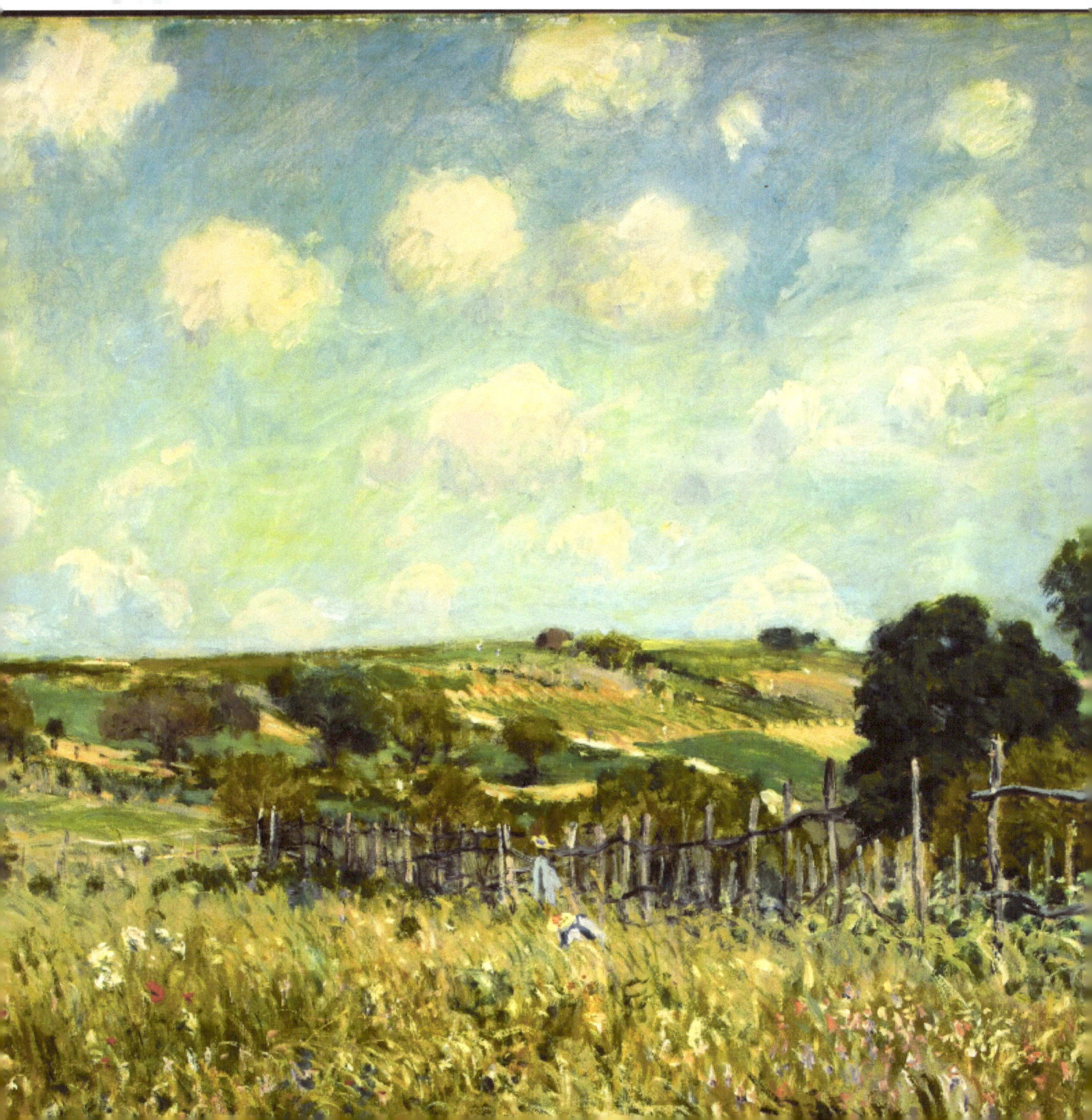

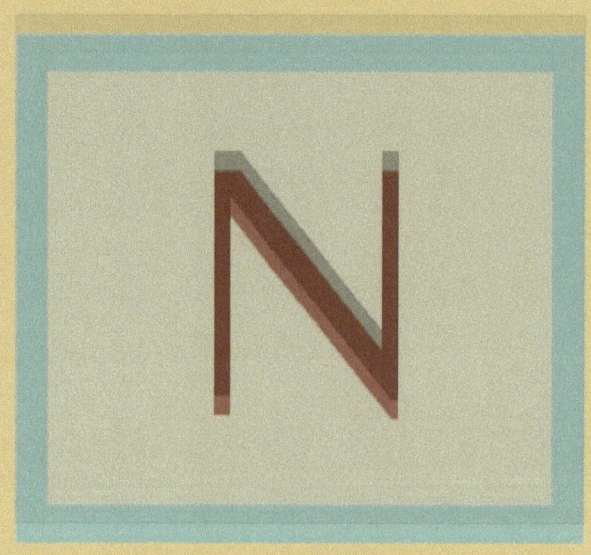

is for nap

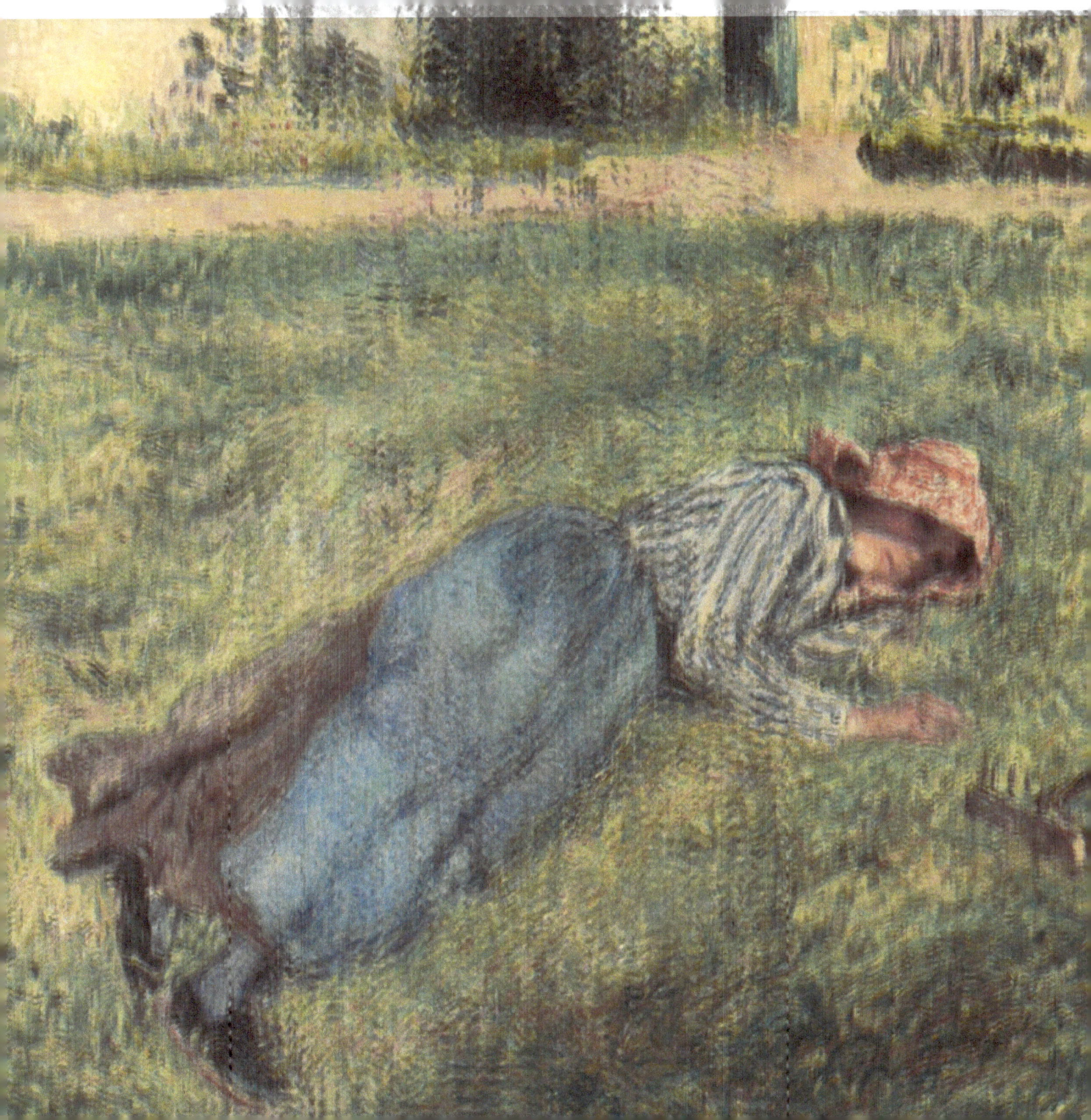

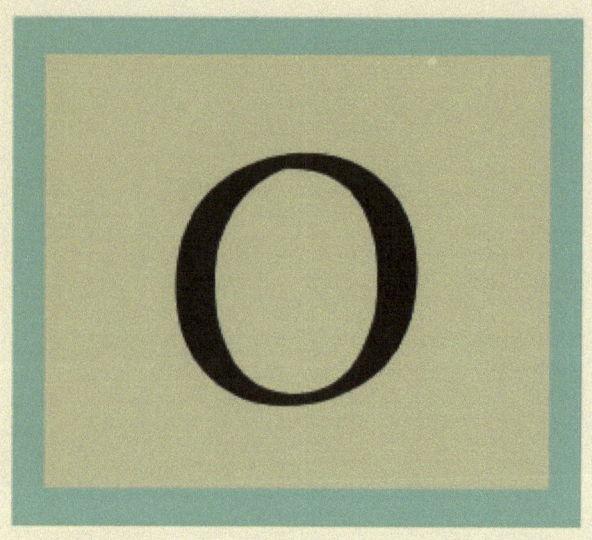

is for old

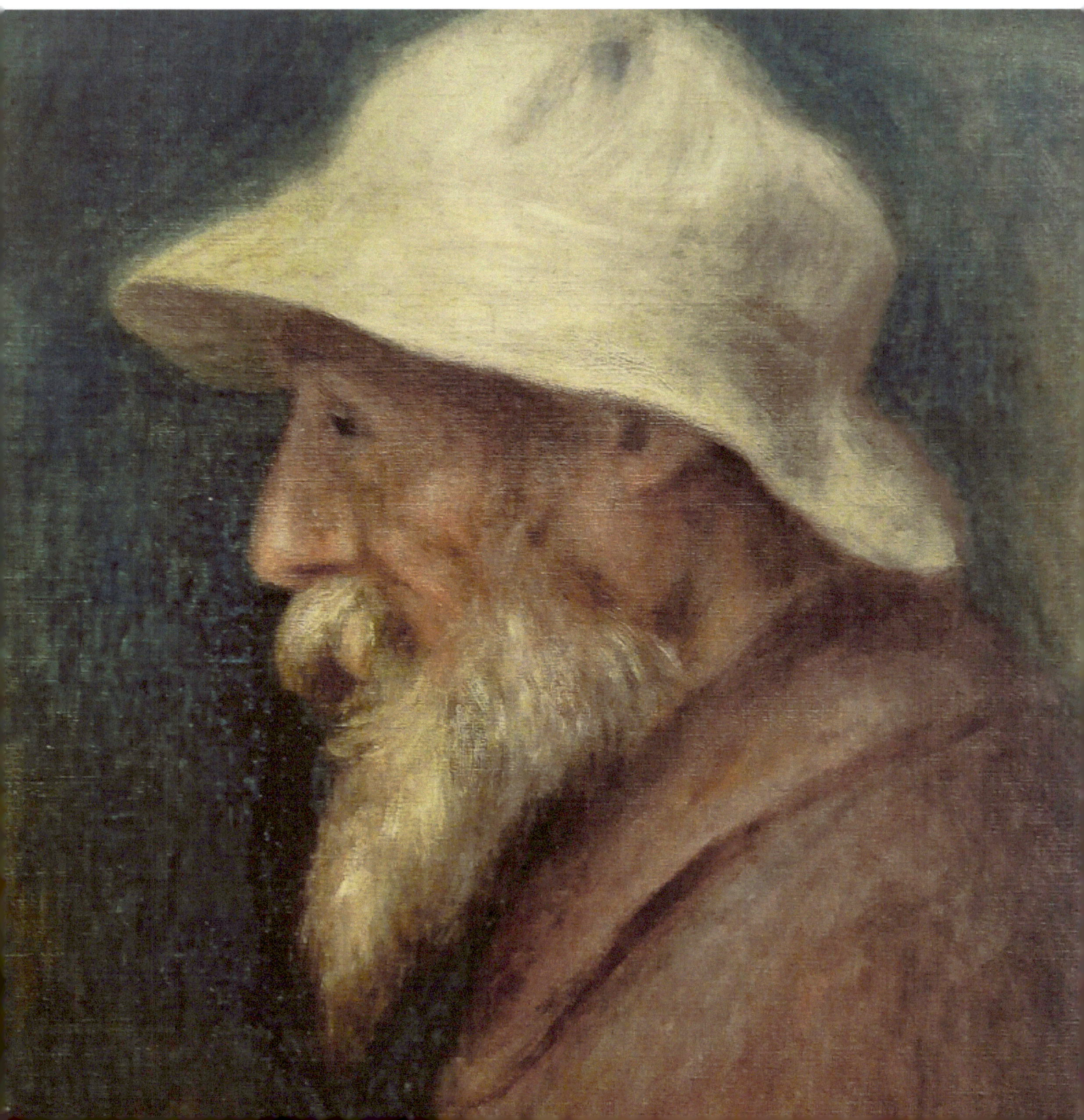

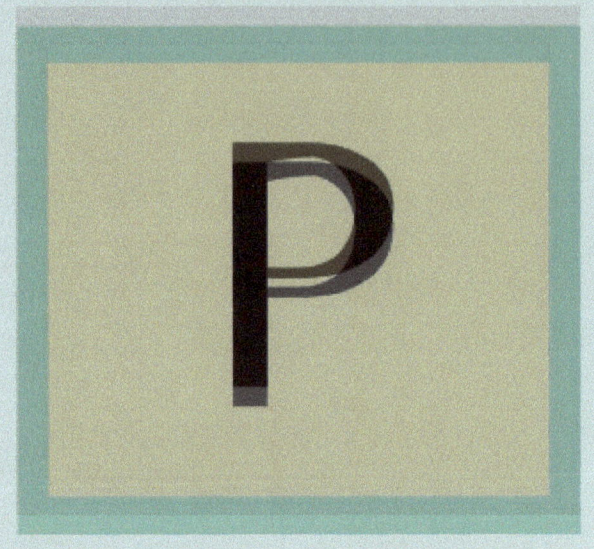

is for path

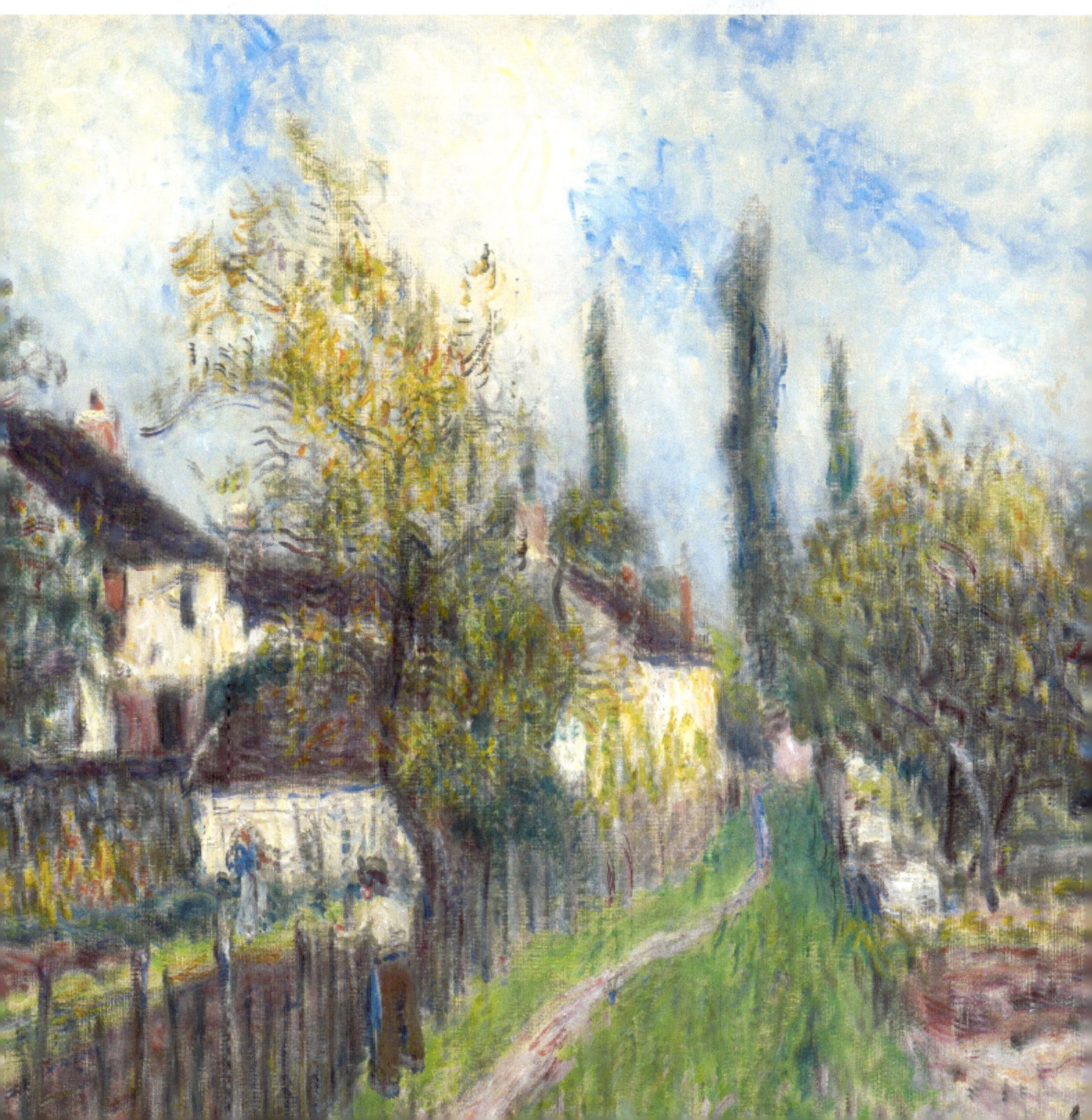

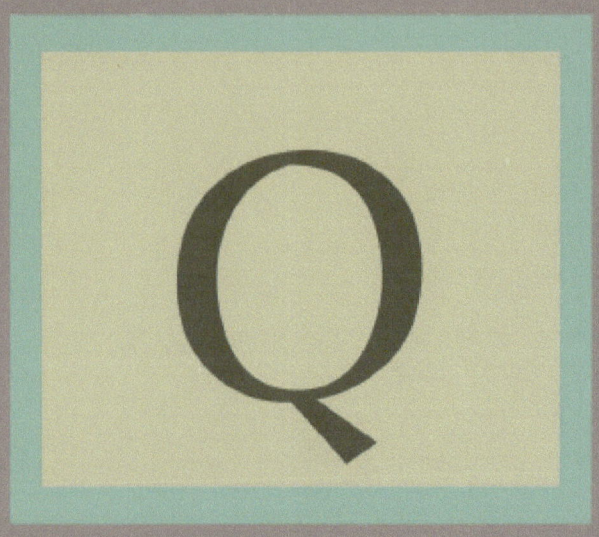

is for quiet

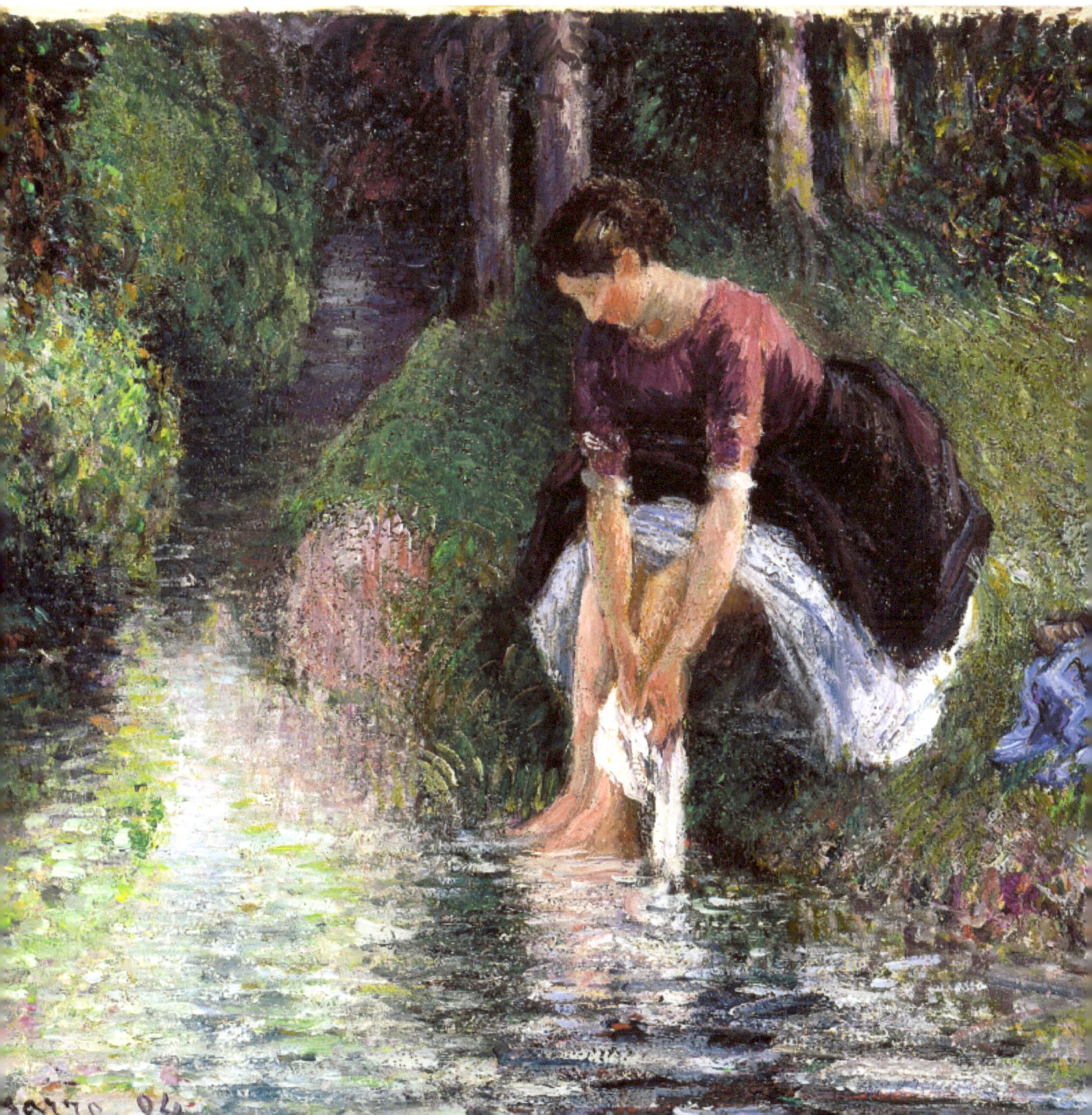

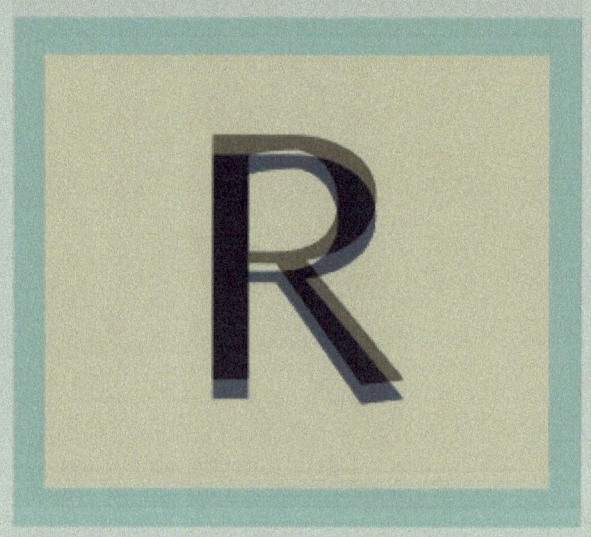

is for row

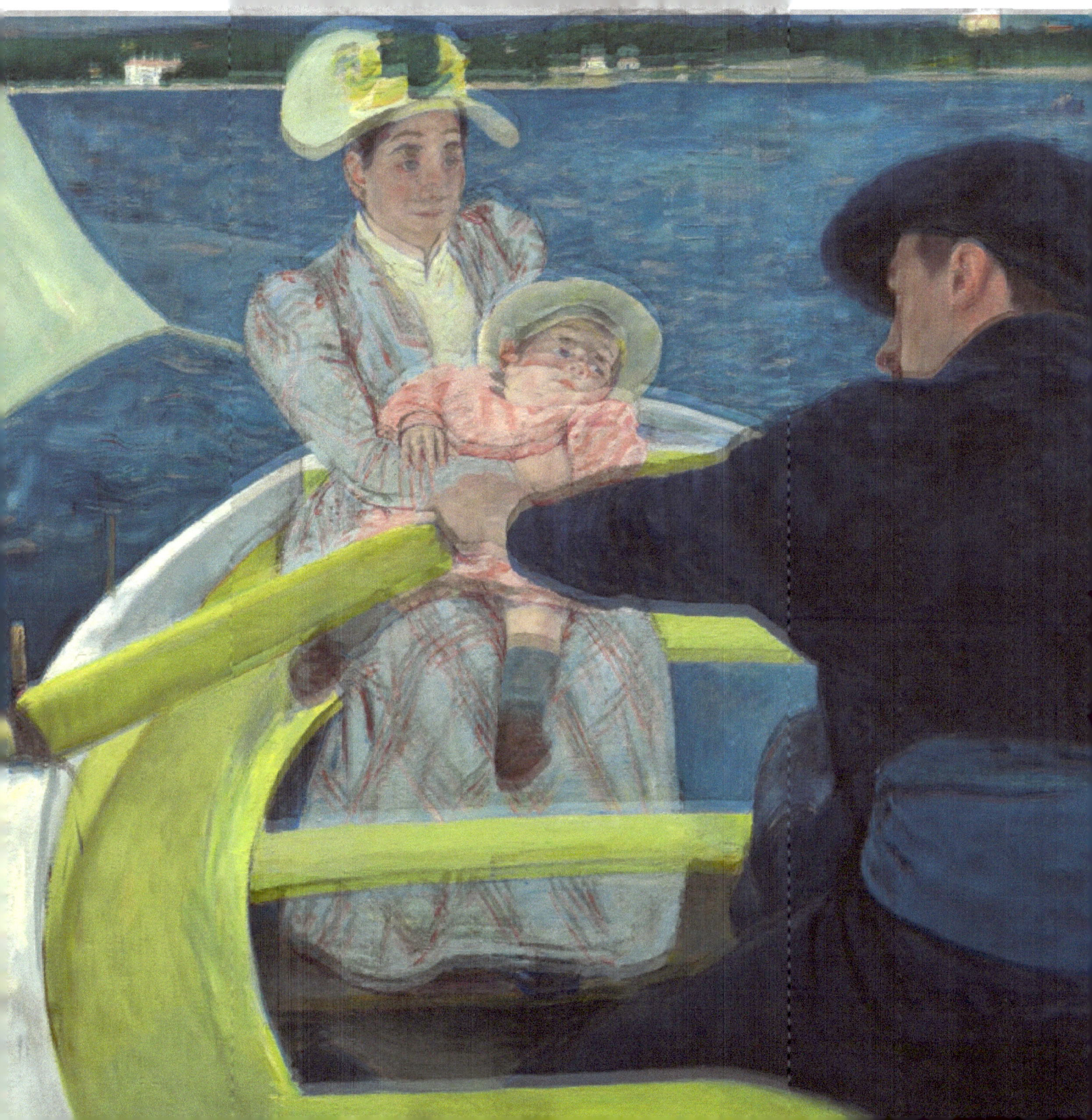

s

is for spaniel

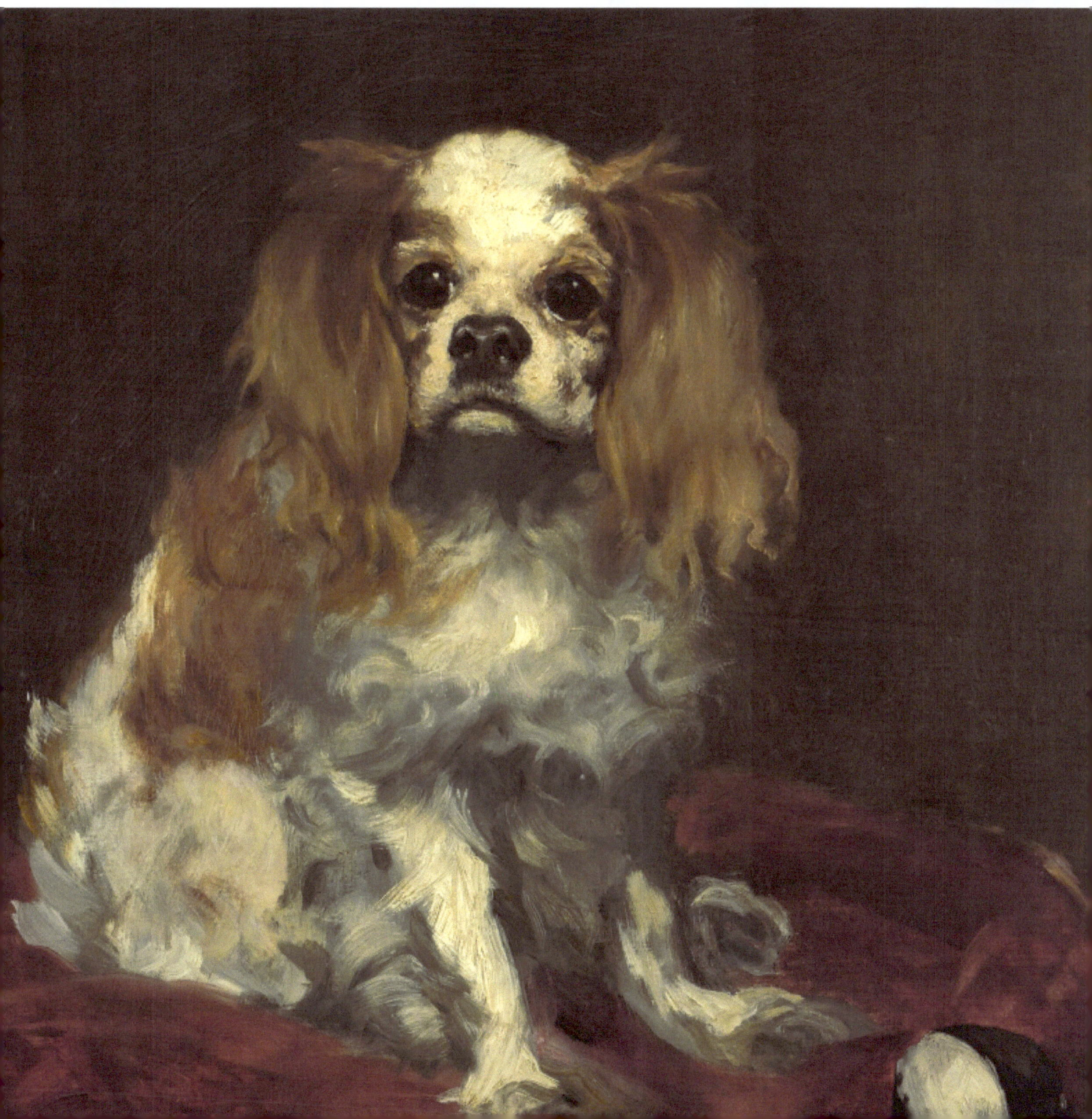

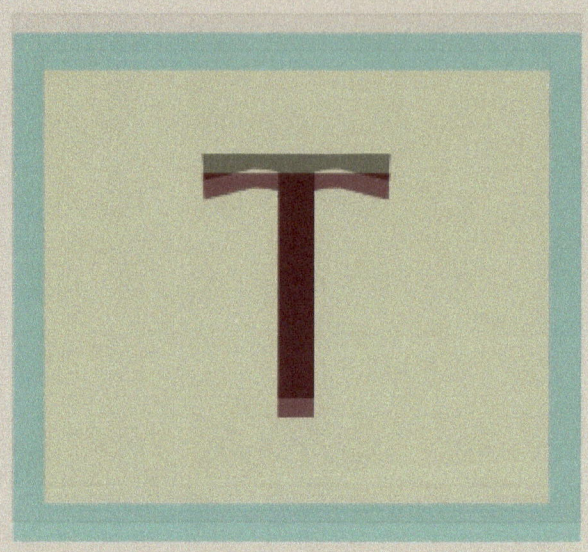

is for theater

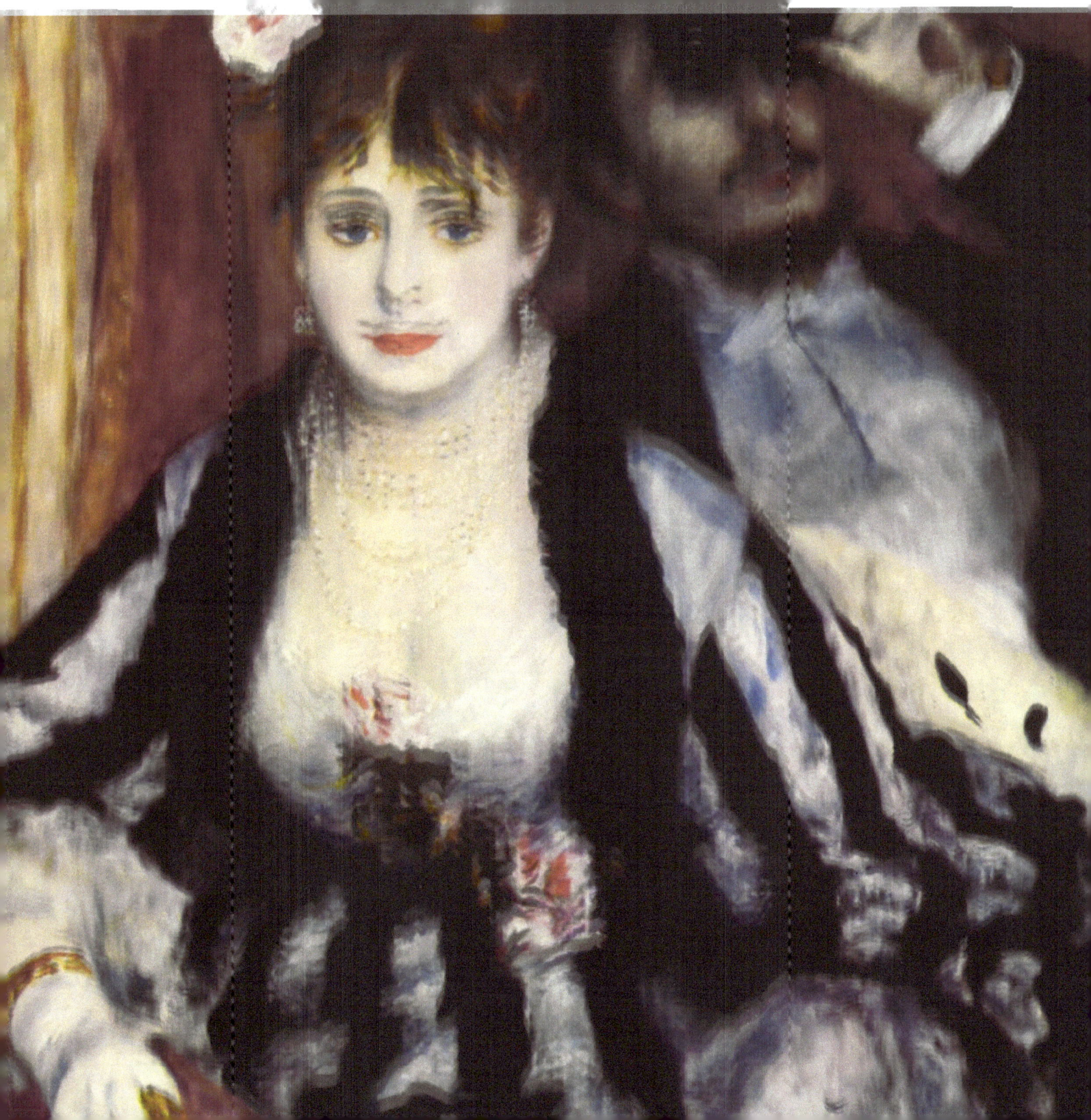

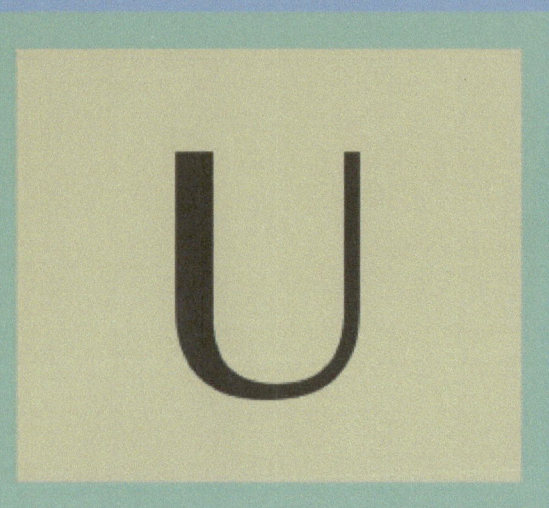

is for umbrella

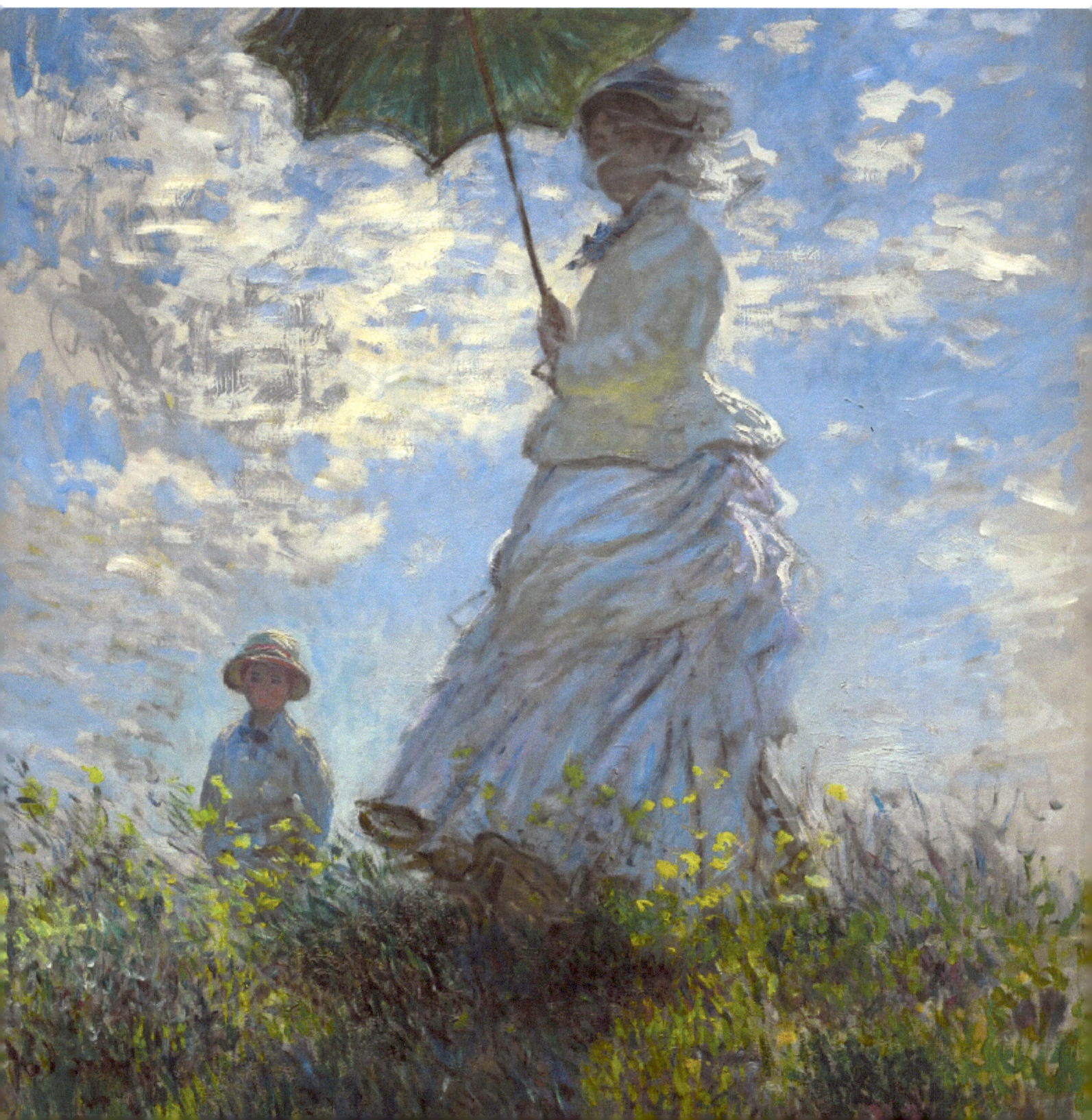

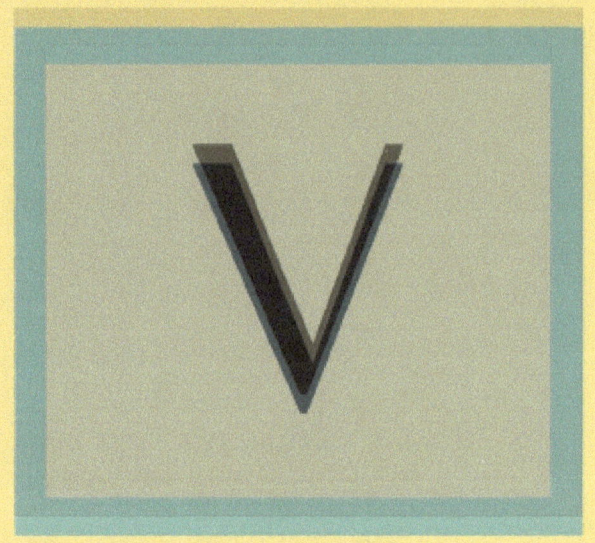

is for vase

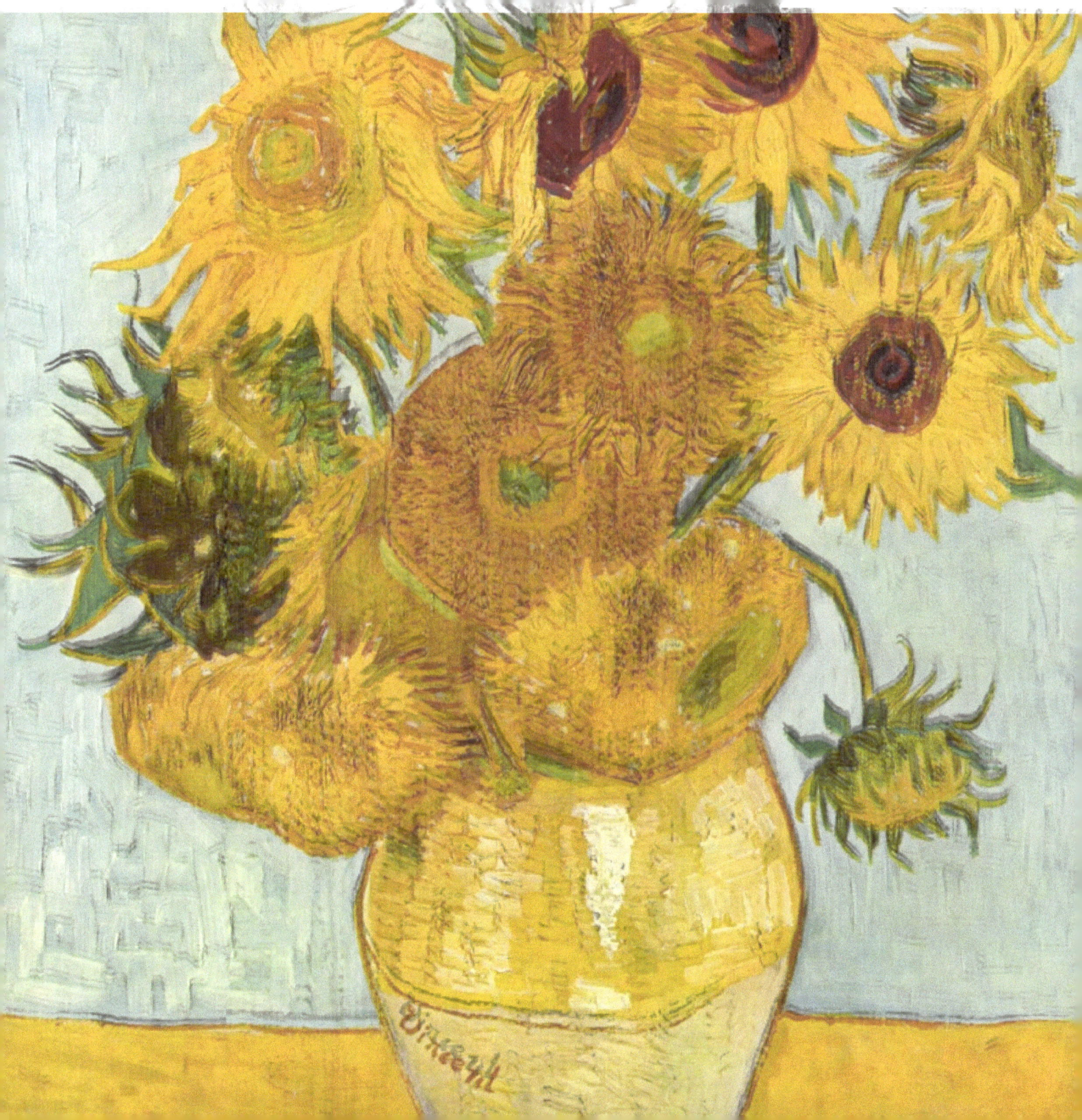

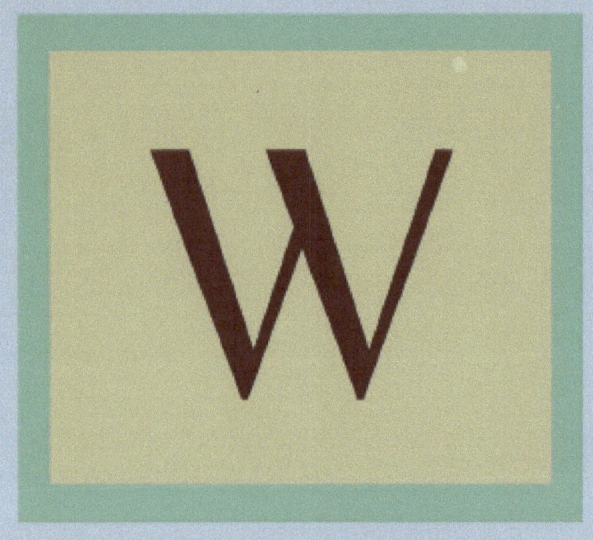

is for water

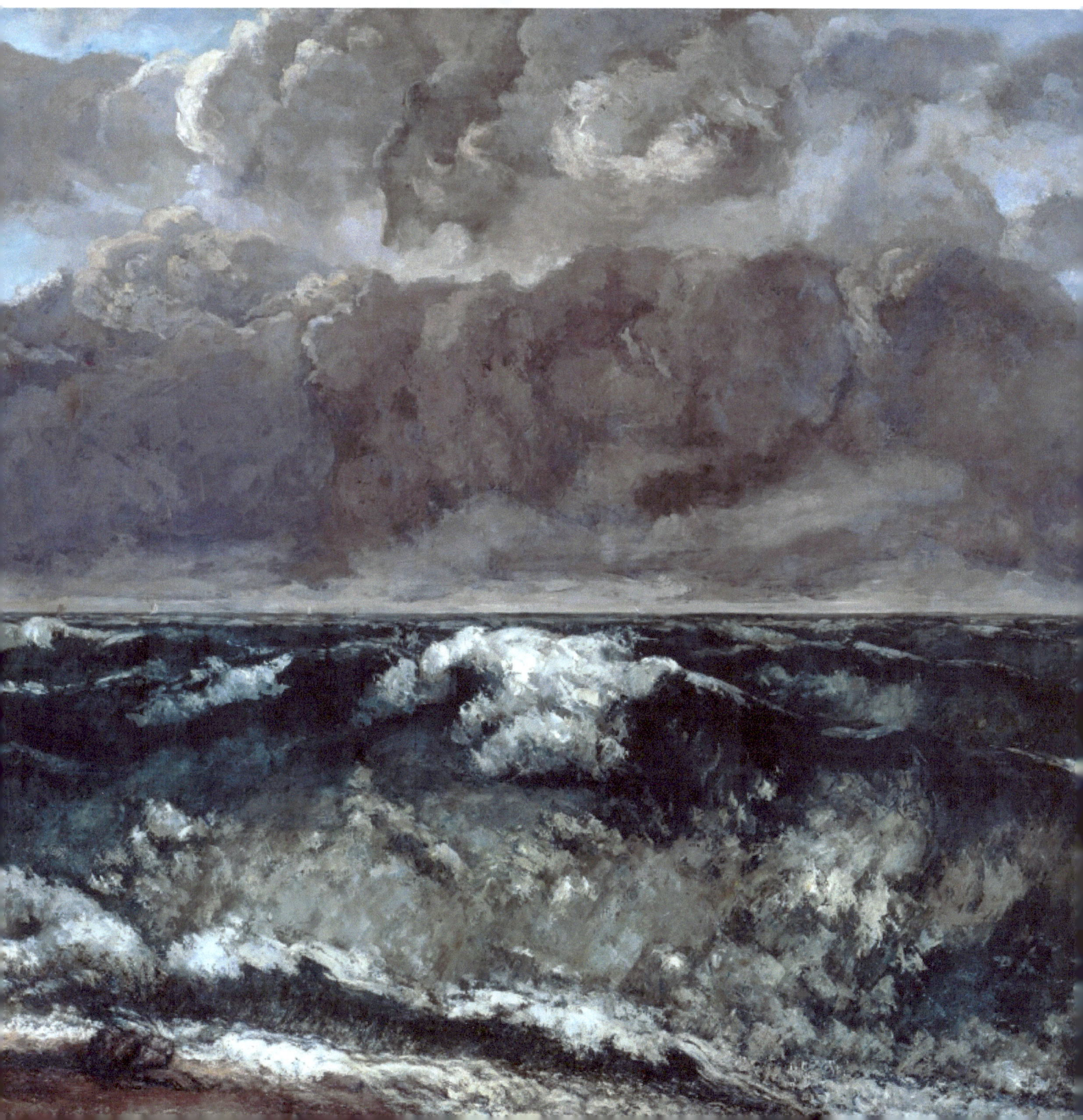

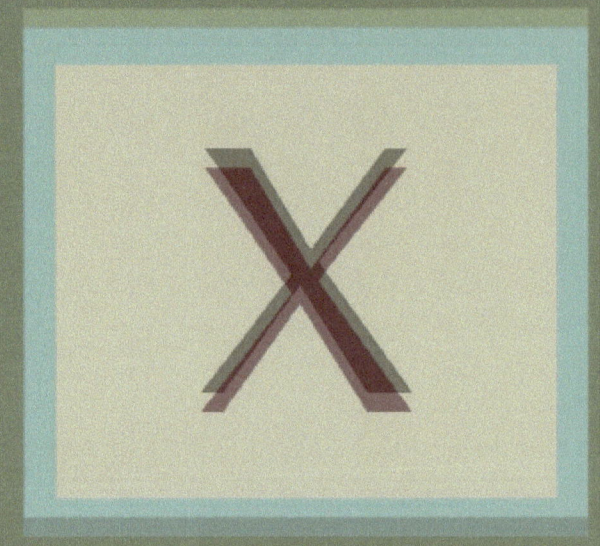

is for eXercise

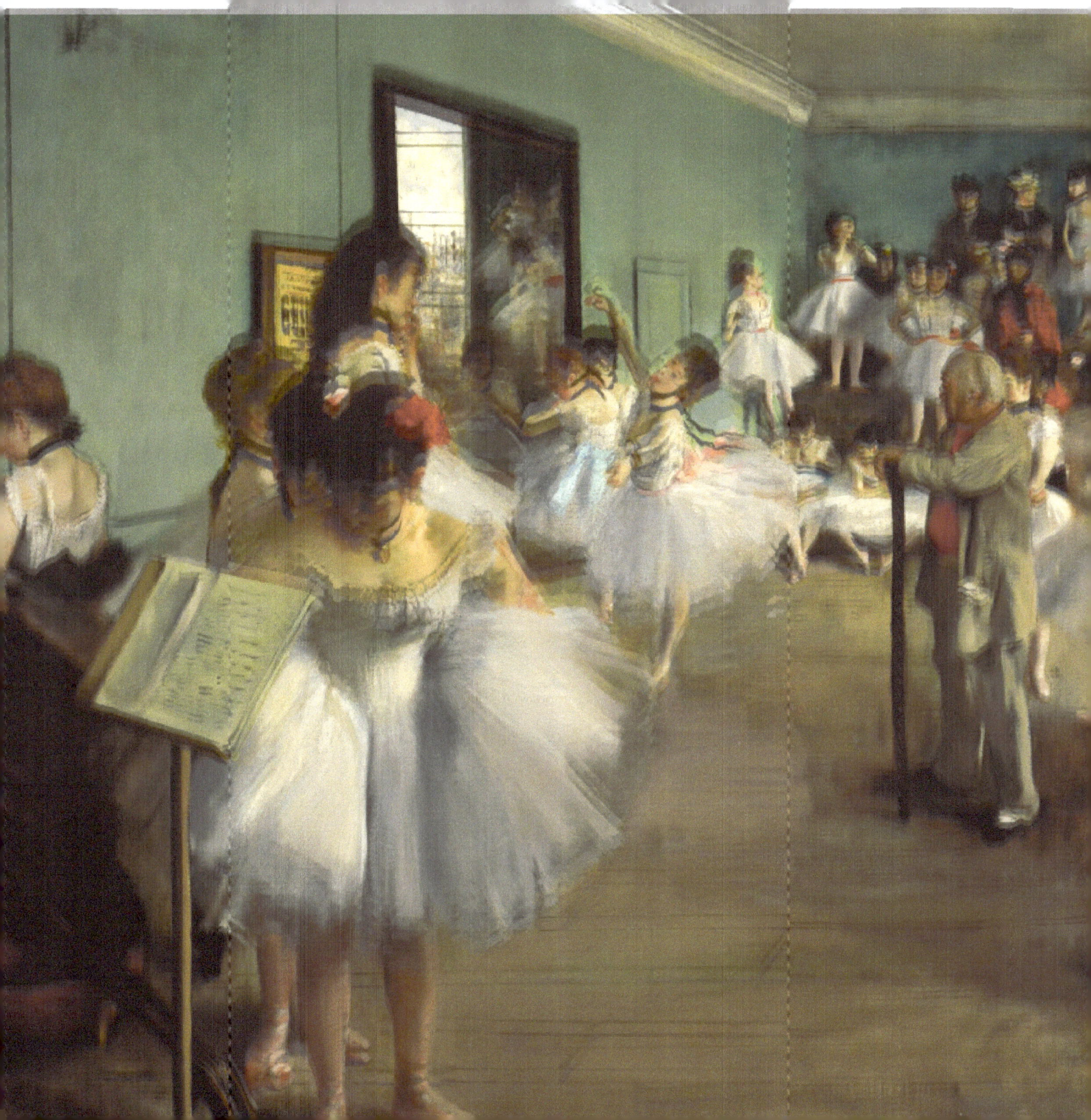

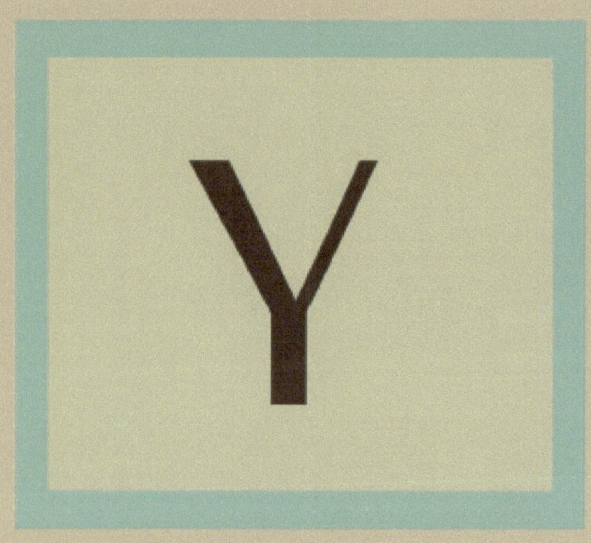

is for young

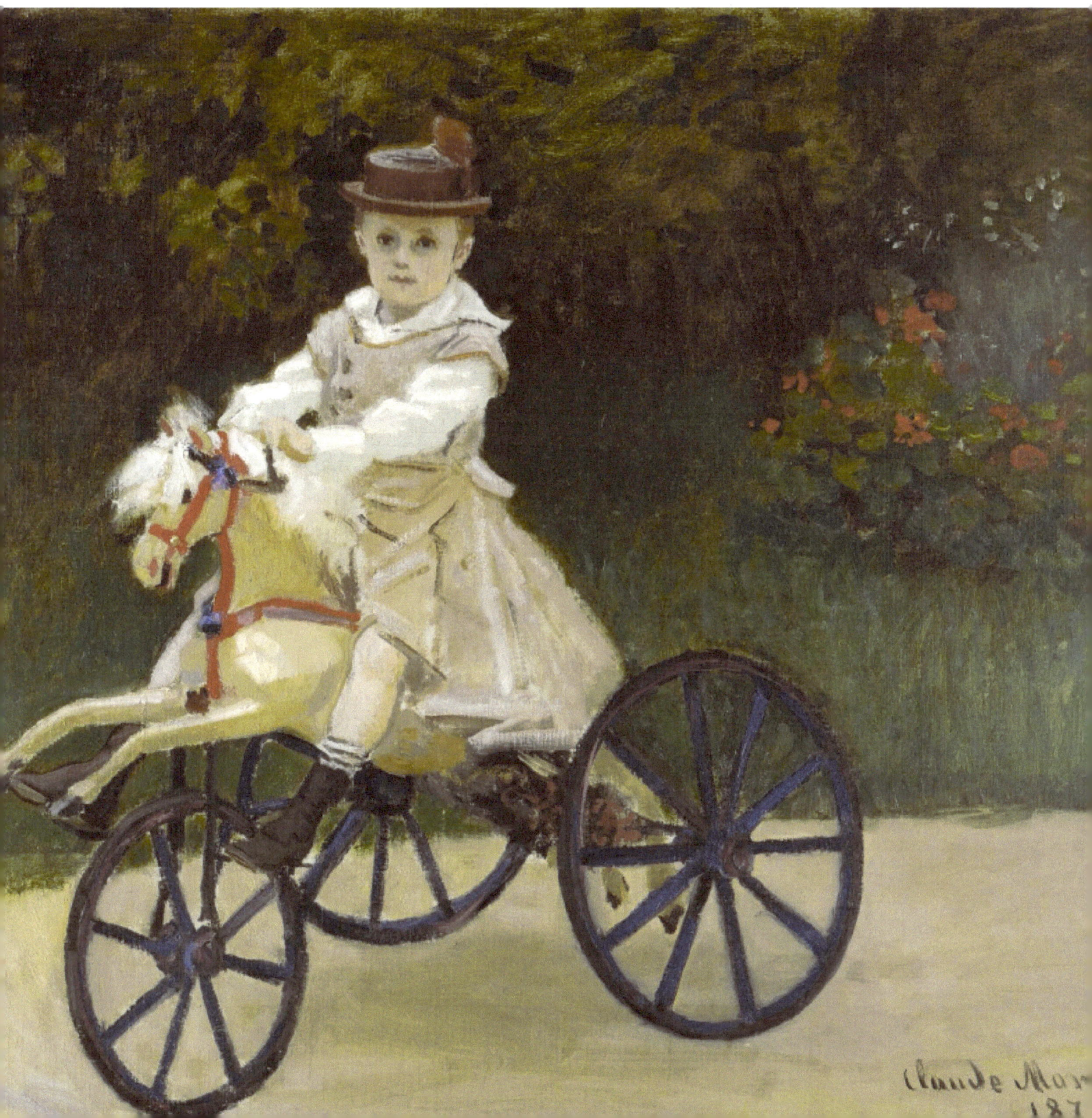

z

is for gaZe

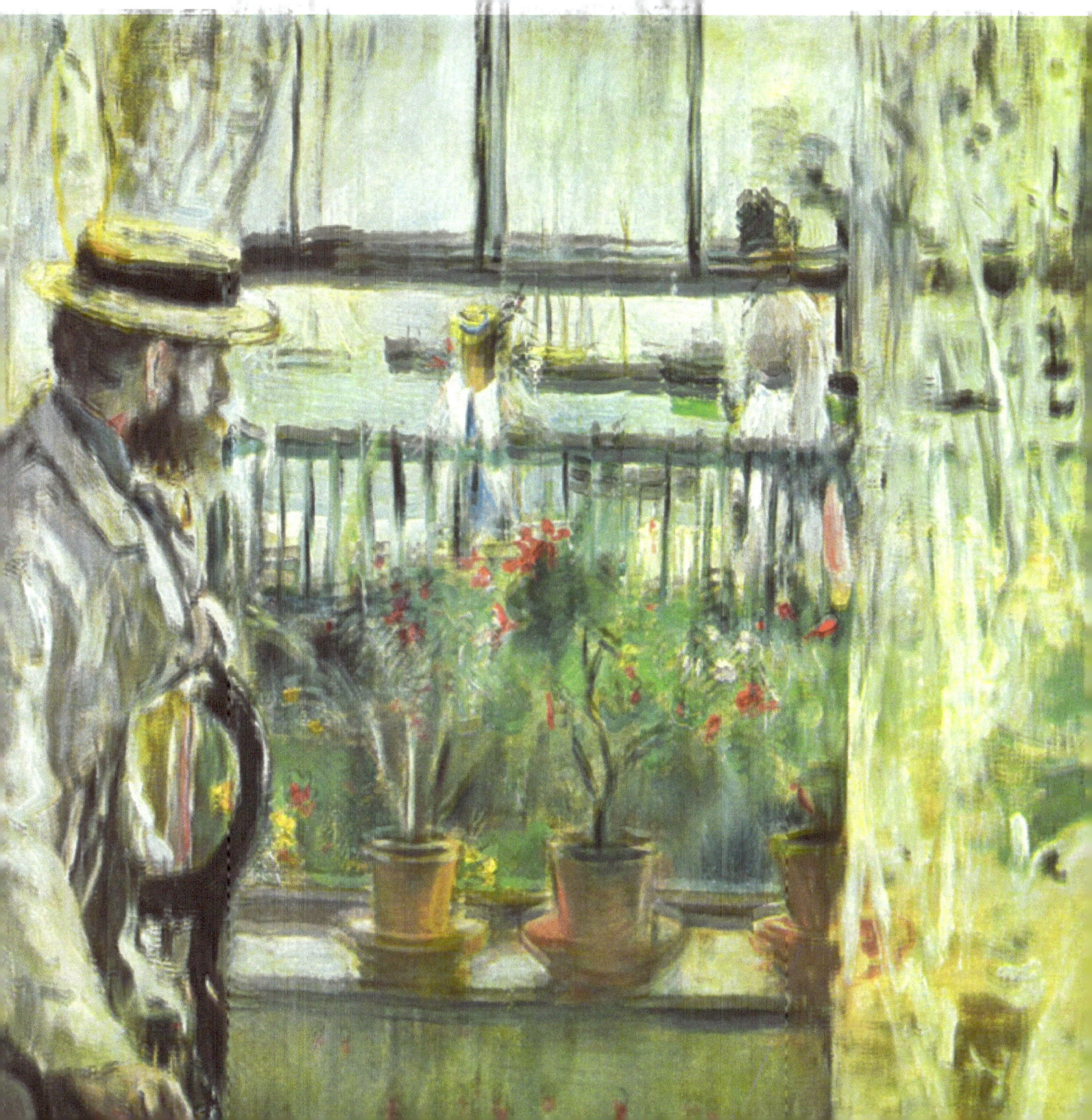

Image credits

———•———

Renoir, Pierre-Auguste. Apples and Flowers. 1895. Hermitage Museum
Cassatt, Mary. The Child's Bath. 1893. Art Institute of Chicago
Morisot, Berthe. The Cradle. 1872. Musée d'Orsay
Monet, Claude. The Luncheon. 1868. Städel Museum
Monet, Claude. Arrival of the Normandy Train, Gare Saint-Lazare. 1877. Art Institute of Chicago
Van Gogh, Vincent. Irises. 1889. J. Paul Getty Museum
Van Gogh, Vincent. Vineyards with a View of Auvers. 1890. Saint Louis Art Museum
Monet, Claude. Grainstack, Sunset. 1891. Museum of Fine Arts, Boston
Monet, Claude. Impression, Sunrise. 1872. Musée Marmottan Monet, Paris
Morisot, Berthe. Summer's Day. 1879. National Portrait Gallery, London.
Morisot, Berthe, In the Dining Room. 1875. National Gallery of Art, Washington D.C.
Van Gogh, Vincent. Still Life of Oranges and Lemons with Blue Gloves.1889. National Gallery of Art
Sisley, Alfred. The Meadow .1875. National Gallery of Art
Pissarro, Camille. The Nap, Peasant Woman Lying in the Grass, Pontoise. 1882. Kunsthalle Bremen
Renoir, Pierre-Auguste. Self Portrait with a White Hat. 1910. Private Collection
Sisley, Alfred. A Path at Les Sablons. 1883. National Gallery of Australia
Pissarro, Camille. Woman Washing Her Feet in a Brook. 1894. Indianapolis Museum of Art
Cassatt, Mary. The Boating Party. 1893. National Gallery of Art, Washington D.C. (post-impressionist)
Manet, Édouard. A King Charles Spaniel. National Gallery of Art, Washington D.C.
Renoir, Pierre-Auguste. The Theatre Box. 1874. Courtauld Gallery, London
Monet, Claude. Woman with a Parasol - Madame Monet and Her Son. 1875. National Gallery of Art, Washington D.C.
Van Gogh, Vincent. Still Life: Vase with Twelve Sunflowers. 1888. Neue Pinakothek, Germany
Courbet, Gustave. The Wave. 1869. National Galleries Scotland
Degas, Edgar. The Dance Class. 1874. Metropolitan Museum of Art
Monet, Claude. Jean Monet on His Hobby Horse. 1872 Metropolitan Museum of Art
Morisot, Berthe Eugène Manet on the Isle of Wight. 1875. Paris, musée Marmottan Monet

FREE
For your budding scholar

Your child can enjoy all the beauty of the Impressionist painters in this free full-color set of ABC cards. Just click on the link below.

https://www.subscribepage.com/g2w6j5

www.ingramcontent.com/pod-product-compliance
Lightning Source LLC
Chambersburg PA
CBHW051922210526
45473CB00006B/2099